EDEXCEL GCSE BUSINESS UNIT 4: INTRODUCTION TO ECONOMIC UNDERSTANDING

Andrew Ashwin

Hodder Arnold

A MEMBER OF THE HODDER HEADLINE GROUP

This material has been endorsed by Edexcel and offers high quality support for the delivery of Edexcel qualifications.

Edexcel endorsement does not mean that this material is essential to achieve any Edexcel qualification, nor does it mean that this is the only suitable material available to support any Edexcel qualification. No endorsed material will be used verbatim in setting any Edexcel examination and any resource lists produced by Edexcel shall include this and other appropriate texts. While this material has been through an Edexcel quality assurance process, all responsibility for the content remains with the publisher.

Copies of official specifications for all Edexcel qualifications may be found on the Edexcel website – www.edexcel.org.uk.

Every effort has been made to trace and acknowledge ownership of copyright. The publishers will be glad to make suitable arrangements with any copyright holders whom it has not been possible to contact. The authors and publishers would like to thank the following for the use of photographs in this volume:

Alamy/Blickwinkel, p78 (right); Alamy/David Hoffmann Photo Library, p80; Alamy/DigitalKnight, p59; Alamy/Kos Picture Source, p78 (left); Alamy/Royan Ong, p112; Alamy/TravelibUK, p67; Corbis/Ant Strack, p1; Corbis/Birgis Allig/Zefa, p77; Corbis/Brian Bailey, p111; Corbis/Scott Olsen/Reuters, p108; Frank Lane Picture Agency/David Hosking, p138; Getty Images/Alex Wong, p126; Innocent Drinks, p38; John Birdsall, p12; Lorna Ainger, p27; PA Photos, p4; PA Photos/Alan Diaz/AP, p122; PA Photos/Claude Paris/AP, p91; PA Photos/Gary Fuller, p35 (top); PA Photos/Johnny Green, p51; PA Photos/Owen Humphreys, p137; PA Photos/Yui Mok, p73; Photofusion/Molly Cooper, p31; Photolibrary/Halaska jacob, p37; Rex Features, pp6, 63; Rex Features/Alex Segre, p57; Rex Features/J.De Tessieres, p133; Rex Features/Matt Baron/BEI, p22; Rex Features/Most Wanted, p42; Rex Features/Ray Tang, p109; Rex Features/Sinopix Photo Agency Ltd, p130; Rex Features/Sipa Press, pp87, 95; Rex Features/Sipa Press/©Succession Picasso/DACS 2007, p35 (bottom); Still Pictures/Hartmut Schwarzbach, p117; Still Pictures/Jordan Schytte, p140; Still Pictures/Tack, p62; The Fairtrade Foundation, p103. The Oxfam logo on p121 is reproduced with the permission of Oxfam GB, Oxfam House, John Smith Drive, Cowley, Oxford OX4 2JY, UK www.oxfam.org.uk. Oxfam GB does [...] company the materials.

Orders: please contact Bookpoint Lt[...] [p]hone: (44) 01235 827720. Fax: (44) 01235 400454. Lines are open from 9.00–5.00, Monday to Saturday, with a 24-hour message answering service. You can also order through our website www.hoddereducation.co.uk.

British Library Cataloguing in Publication Data
A catalogue record for this title is available from the British Library

ISBN: 978 0 340 94179 9
First Published 2007
Impression number   10 9 8 7 6 5 4 3 2 1
Year   2012 2011 2010 2009 2008 2007

Copyright © 2007 Andrew Ashwin

Cover photo © Fred Lyon/Science Photo Library
Typeset by Fakenham Photosetting Ltd, Fakenham, Norfolk
Illustrations by Barking Dog Art
Printed in Italy for Hodder Arnold, an imprint of Hodder Education and a member of the Hodder Headline Group, an Hachette Livre UK Company, 338 Euston Road, London NW1 3BH

Contents

Acknowledgements

I would like to thank all the students that I have taught over the years who have contributed so much to my thinking about learning in economics without ever realising it. Thanks are also due to Ian Marcousé who has been a valued critical friend in the development of the specification and the writing of this book. At Hodder, Anita Gaspar and Deborah Edwards have been highly supportive, thank you. Thanks also to my Mum – not quite the book my teachers told her I would write, but a book nevertheless! Finally, thanks to Sue, Alex and Jonathan for their support and love

SECTION 1

THINKING LIKE
AN ECONOMIST

1 The economic problem

Introduction to economics

You are about to start on a journey into the subject of economics. You may not have much idea of what 'economics' is about except that it's something to do with money. Certainly, money plays a very big part in economics. But it's about much more than that.

When we hear the word 'money', we usually imagine cash – the bits of paper and metal that we use to get the things we **want** and **need**. Money represents spending power. If we go to a shop to get a chocolate bar or a piece of fruit, we use cash to buy the items we want. Money is a **means of exchange**.

At this point, there is a basic problem that we need to consider:

■ We tend to have many wants. If you were asked to write down a list of the things that you would like to own, how long would it take you? It might take quite a long time because the list of things you want could be long one. However, (and here is the problem)…

■ We tend to have limited finances. Most of us do not have an endless amount of money to buy all the things on our lists.

It's just the same for businesses. Governments, too, are always talking about not being able to afford to do everything they want to do. As for the world, you will have noticed all the problems: starving children, poverty, war, famine, disease, hunger, drought. If we had enough money, we think, then surely we could solve them all?

Money allows us to buy **resources**. Resources are all the things that allow us to be able to satisfy our wants and needs. Resources are things like oil, metals, minerals, timber, water, machinery, equipment, food, buildings, human labour and so on.

The problem is that we do not have unlimited resources to meet all our wants and needs. As a result we have to make choices. Economics is all about how we make **choices** between different things.

Revision Essentials

A need is something necessary for our survival – food, water, clothing, shelter, warmth and so on.

A want is something we would like to have but which is not essential for our survival (for example, a new games console, mobile phone or that jacket in Top Shop)

Resources enable us to satisfy our wants and needs. There are usually not enough resources to do everything. When this happens, resources are termed scarce resources.

Choices are the decisions we have to make because of scarce resources.

If we look at news headlines we can see examples of the economic problem in action. Here are some examples:

- British Airways announce higher profits.
- Oil Prices set rise to over $100 a barrel.
- Rock star Bono in plan to promote fair trade for Africa.
- Music industry hit by new bands using the Internet.
- 2012 ticket demand outstrips supply.
- Private schools reprimanded by competition watchdog.
- NHS to send patients abroad for treatment.
- Immigration vital for industry, says minister.
- World trade talks reach stalemate.
- Cholera epidemic sweeps Angolan slums.
- UK shoppers stay away from high street.
- UK top of 'fat charts'.

Each of these news headlines hides a story. At the heart of the story will be the problem of unlimited wants and needs, scarce resources and the need to make choices.

Exercises

In groups of three, discuss what you think the economic issues are behind the news headlines in the list above. Write a short paragraph summarising your ideas. Share your ideas with the rest of your class. What differences are there in the ideas you have covered?

Exercises

1 Write down ten things that you would like to buy if you had the opportunity.
2 How much money do you have to spend each week, on average?
3 Can you afford to buy all the ten things you have written down?
4 Of the ten things you have written down, what can you afford to buy with your money (income)?
5 If you were told you could choose just **one** of the ten items, which would you choose?
6 Explain why you chose that item rather than any other on your list.

Revision Essentials
The economic problem is that we have unlimited wants and needs but limited or scarce resources.

Economists are always asking questions and seeking answers. They might be very important questions like:

- How do we best deal with the problem of poverty in Africa and other parts of the world?
- How might we reduce the damage we are doing to the planet?

These are problems that are international in nature. We might also be concerned with more local problems such as:

- Why we can't make sure that all schools have access to the books and equipment they need?
- Why can't the Council afford to keep the local youth club open?

The questions could be about very ordinary things, like:

- Why is this packet of crisps 40p? Why not 35p or 45p?
- Why do we always get stuck in traffic on a Friday afternoon at 4.30pm?
- Why does the supermarket have checkouts that are not open when there are queues of people waiting to pay?

Everywhere we go there are questions. Economists ask questions all the time about these issues. They are curious to know more about how the world works in the way it does. Sometimes we might question things that do not seem to be very logical.

- How do we have flooding and water shortages at the same time?
- Why does the government keep going on about reducing greenhouse gases yet supports the building of an aeroplane that carries up to 800 people?
- Why is a pair of Nike trainers so expensive compared to other non-branded trainers?
- Why do people replace their perfectly good mobile phones with newer ones?

Why do we have congestion on the roads? Just one of the many questions economists ask

We might keep asking questions but there is little point if we can't find any answers. There are, of course, answers to most things, but the ones we get might not always be the ones we want to hear, or ones we would agree with.

Economists look at issues and try to find answers in the following ways. They think about:

- how resources are used
- scarcity
- choices
- value.

They ask about:

- who has power
- how systems work
- if there are 'better' ways to do things.

This is your economist's thinking toolkit. As we go through this book, these issues will become clearer. It will be worth coming back to this page from time to time and asking what relevance these questions have to the issues and problems that we cover.

Exercises

Write down what you think might be the answers to the questions below. Don't worry if you don't really know – often the experts don't really know either! One of the key things about thinking like an economist is to be prepared to make mistakes but to learn from them. One of the great (and sometimes frustrating) things about economics is that there are no 'correct' answers. A good way to learn is to start with what you know and build from there, so write down whatever you can come up with.

1 Why is a packet of supermarket own-brand cereal much cheaper than brand-named cereals like **Kelloggs**?
2 Why is a Kit Kat 37p?
3 Why do we pay for bottled water when we can get it out of the tap?
4 What do we mean when we say something is 'expensive'?
5 Why do some people earn massive amounts of money when others earn very little?

2 The importance of perspectives

Right or wrong?

Read this conversation between three friends about the cause of greenhouse gases and the possible solutions.

'The way to reduce greenhouse gases that are harming the planet is to cut down the number of plane journeys we make.'

'Rubbish – the way to solve the problem is to cut the amount of cars on the road.'

'You're both wrong, it is energy companies that are the biggest polluters – electricity companies and the like – they should be taxed to stop them doing it!'

In some respects, they are all correct about sources of greenhouse gases, but that does not mean that the solutions they suggest would solve the problem. Most issues in economics do not have one simple answer. Often, there are many different reasons for something and there is also likely to be a choice of different possible solutions.

You will have heard about people arguing about all sorts of issues that occur every day. In 2005, Bob Geldof organised a series of concerts called **Live 8** to raise awareness about poverty. He wanted to put pressure on world leaders to address the problem at a summit meeting being held in Scotland. Many people praised Geldof for what he was trying to do. There were also plenty of people who criticised him, most

The organisers of Live 8

notably some people who live in some of the countries that Geldof was trying to help. They saw the Live 8 concerts as merely an opportunity for Geldof to boost his own image and reputation and not being about helping reduce poverty.

In the winter of 2005, gas prices rose dramatically. Industrial users of gas found their costs for energy rising by over 100 per cent, while domestic users of gas for heating and cooking also saw their bills rise by nearly 25 per cent. At the same time, the companies producing gas seemed to be making bigger profits. Surely this was not right?

After a review into the UK's long-term energy requirements, the British Prime Minister came down in support of expanding the use of nuclear fuel as a means of providing for our energy needs. This view was criticised by many as being too expensive, too dangerous and not taking into account the value of renewable energy such as solar and wind power.

These three scenarios show that different people have different views (**perspectives**) on the same issue. They highlight the differences of opinion that can exist over the same issues.

Economists have to deal with differences of opinion all the time. For example, a hospital might announce that it has to cut jobs in order to reduce its costs and cut the losses it is making. It says that the job cuts will be associated with a reduction in the number of beds but that the cuts will not affect how well patients are cared for.

Trades Unions, who represent the views of employees and who are representing the staff at this hospital, might have a different perspective. They might argue that these cuts will have a devastating effect on patient care. If you have fewer nurses and fewer beds then it seems logical that fewer people will receive the sort of treatment and care that they need and expect.

So who is right, and what does the economist do about it? The answer in most of these cases is that neither perspective is 'right' but that there might be some element of truth in both views. The economist will try and find out what the **facts** are and separate them from the **opinion**.

Revision Essentials

A fact is something that can be supported by some evidence. For example, if I said that Notts County Football Club has won more trophies in its history than Manchester United, a quick look at the evidence would tell you that this claim is simply not true.

An opinion is something that cannot either be proved or disproved by reference to any evidence. 'Notts County are the best football team in the country' is an example of an opinion. It is my view and belief. How I define 'best' might cover a whole host of things (e.g. quality of tackling, spectacular defence) but I am entitled to my opinion, just as your have every right to yours.

Perspectives are the different opinions held by people on the same issue.

Exercise

Below is an extract from information provided by energy company **ScottishPower** in May 2006. ScottishPower provides gas and electricity to customers in their homes and to businesses. It raised gas prices by 15 per cent in March 2006 and electricity prices by 8 per cent. It warned that further price increases in energy were inevitable in the coming year.

Philip Bowman, ScottishPower Chief Executive, said:

'This is an excellent set of results for ScottishPower. All our businesses have delivered very good growth through improved operational performance and attractive returns on our investment programme. With the sale of PacifiCorp completed, ScottishPower now has a strong set of businesses that are well positioned in their markets and offer attractive prospects for future growth. I am confident that ScottishPower will continue to make significant progress and create value for shareholders.'

- Cash generated from continuing operations increased by £183m to £864m.
- Continuing businesses capital investment of £1bn; 67 per cent for growth, principally UK and US windfarms.
- Continuing businesses deliver strong profit growth.
- Adjusted operating profit £805m (up 39 per cent).
- Adjusted profit before tax £675m (up 47 per cent).

(Source: www.scottishpower.com)

Take a piece of paper and divide the page into two columns – one headed 'Fact' and other 'Opinion'. Look at the sentences from the article and write them in the relevant column. Don't worry too much if you don't fully understand all that is being said – that is not the object here. Remember that facts can be supported by reference to some sort of evidence, whereas opinion cannot be 'proved'.

What evidence is there that reducing hospital staff and beds will not affect patient care? Let's look at some of the things people say about this:

- More people could be treated at home or in drop-in centres, for example, rather than staying in hospital.
- The hospital might find ways of reducing the need for beds – by reducing the time that people have to stay in hospital.
- A reduction in the number of beds might help to reduce the number of people who get ill in hospitals because they get nasty bugs while in hospital!

To investigate the facts, we might want to look at cases where the number of nurses has been reduced and to see what the response of patients has been. Have people been more ill for longer as a result? Do they feel that their care has been worse?

By doing this type of investigation, we can try to get a clearer picture of what the true position is and this allows us to be able to make a recommendation or decision about what to do. The answer might lie somewhere in the middle of the two perspectives.

Making decisions

Economists have to understand that there are often emotional issues involved in arguments such as this. These issues can lead us to making decisions that may not always be the best. By investigating the facts, economists are able to see things from different perspectives.

The solution to a problem might not always be something that we like. For example, if we want to reduce traffic congestion, one of the obvious ways is to make people pay for the privilege of using the roads. At the moment we only pay a part of the true cost of using the road when we get into our cars. We are not aware of how expensive it is to build and maintain roads.

If I offered you my mobile phone to use as much as you like for just 10p a day, you would almost certainly think it was a good deal. If you had an offer like this, the chances are that you would overuse the phone. That is exactly what is happening with our roads, as they are relatively cheap to use. However, if I changed the rules and asked you to pay 50p every time you used my phone, then you would be likely to use it far less.

With roads, one of the solutions is to make people more aware of the true price of using the roads and make them pay more. If you suggest this to your parents, my guess is that they may see the logic, but they may not like the idea. They might have a different perspective.

Economists' solutions are not always 'nice' solutions. The politicians are the ones who have to sell some of these ideas to the public. However, since politicians rely on the public for their jobs they are sometimes unwilling to put unpopular solutions into action.

Exercise

Look at the following short examples.

- A disused wall outside a local community centre has been covered in graffiti by some local youths. This example of street art is being discussed by the local council who are planning to have it removed.
- A local hospital is planning to increase the charges for parking in its car parks from 20p per hour to 40p. One of the local papers is outraged by this and is starting a campaign against the plans.
- A business is investigating a site on which to locate a small wind farm. The wind farm consists of ten wind turbines. The energy needs of two local housing estates will be met by the project but some local residents are concerned that the wind farms might be noisy and reduce the value of their properties.

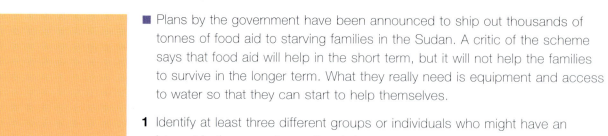

■ Plans by the government have been announced to ship out thousands of tonnes of food aid to starving families in the Sudan. A critic of the scheme says that food aid will help in the short term, but it will not help the families to survive in the longer term. What they really need is equipment and access to water so that they can start to help themselves.

1 Identify at least three different groups or individuals who might have an interest in the scenarios outlined above.
2 Explain the different perspectives that each group or individual might have about the scenario.

3   Scarcity

One thing an economist learns about very early on is scarcity. This might not be obvious in the relative luxury of living in the UK, which is one of the world's richest countries. The vast majority of the population in the UK have somewhere to live and access to running water and heating; regular meals; a car or other transport; enough clothing; and enjoy a range of leisure activities.

Even in the UK, however, we do have scarcity. Everything has a limit, it is just that some things are more scarce than others. Scarcity does not mean a great deal unless you link it to **wants** and **needs**. As human beings, we all have some basic wants and needs (including food, clothing and shelter). These needs have to be satisfied on a regular basis.

Other needs are less frequent; for example, I need a mobile phone. Well, that's not exactly true, I *want* a mobile phone. However, once I have bought one, I will not need to buy another for a least a year or two. You might think that food manufacturers would be in a strong position, given our daily need for food. Mobile phone manufacturers face a different problem. After all, if everyone over the age of 13 in the UK had a mobile phone, would that mean that they do not have to produce any more mobile phones?

To make sense of scarcity we need to relate it to our wants and needs. We know that a need is something that is vital to our survival. A

want is something we would like to have but that is not necessary for our survival. (I want a 32-inch plasma screen TV and a full Sky sports and movies package but if I do not get it my life will not be in danger – I do not *need* it.)

The problem arises when our wants and needs are unlimited. It does not matter how much money you have got, there is always something else to buy. David Beckham has millions of pounds, yet still finds things to spend it on. He might choose to spend half a million pounds hosting a party for friends and team mates. Many of us would probably think that spending that sort of money on a party is excessive. For David Beckham it might be that this is 'small change' compared to the amount he earns.

In May 2006, a Picasso painting was sold at auction for over £52 million. The unknown winning bidder clearly had plenty of money! Who knows how far they might have been prepared to go in the bidding process?

Compare those cases to a single mum with two children, living in a flat on a council estate. She has a very limited income – less than £200 a week – and has to pay for food, rent, clothing, heating and lighting as well as meeting the demands of her children. She does not have much chance to go out and socialise. She has got a job but has to work part time because she has to care for her children. Child care is also expensive.

Some people have barely enough to live on, even in a developed country like the UK

If we expand our investigation to looking at other aspects of scarcity we can see that there are plenty of examples of scarce resources. Oil, gas, coal, copper, land, water – all these are scarce resources. In the case of oil there are billions of barrels of oil reserves still in the earth but the problem is that we are using oil in increasing amounts. One day, it must run out.

Our conclusion to all this is that all resources are scarce – but they are scarce in relation to the fact that we all want more and more. We say that resources are scarce in relation to the demand for them. We want more than there is available.

Exercise

Think about these different situations, which involve scarcity.

- If a new oil field with billions of barrels of oil was discovered in the Atlantic Ocean, would oil still be a scarce resource?
- There is a saying: 'Water, water everywhere but not a drop to drink.' Why do we have to pay for water if there is so much of it?
- In recent years, the price of copper has risen dramatically. In 2001, a tonne of copper could be bought for around £780; in 2006, a tonne of copper would set you back £3,900. Why do you think the price has risen so much?
- At the end of a busy car boot sale, Jane and Steph still have 20 CDs that they have not sold. They lower the price from £2 to £1 but still don't manage to sell any. The crowds are starting to drift away. They lower the price to 50p but only manage to persuade one person to buy one. Does this mean that these CDs are not scarce?

Investigation

Could you live on £200 per week? Try to find out how much the rent on an average council flat is, how much gas and electricity bills are, how much an average family might spend on food each week, how much child care is, and the cost of transport and clothing. Can you survive on £200?

4   Choice

The existence of the **economic problem** means that we have to make choices. Whenever you go to the shops you have to make choices. Businesses also have to make choices, and so do governments, international bodies and institutions.

Imagine that you have been given money by friends and family for your birthday and that you have £100 to spend. You head off into town with some friends for a shopping binge. You wander round the shops and see loads of things you would like to buy – there is a really good MP3 player that you would like, there are plenty of clothes that take your fancy, some cool shoes, several DVDs and some sports equipment you have been looking for.

So much to choose from, so little money!

The problem now is how to allocate your scarce resources (spend your money). You might like to buy all the things that you see, but you have a limit of £100. So you have to make some choices:

- If you buy the MP3 player you want, it will take up most of your £100.
- If you go for the clothes, then you can get quite a few different items with your £100.
- You could go for the shoes and have enough left for some DVDs.
- You could choose some other combination.

What do you decide to do?

Who will pay for the extra police time? Is it the best way of solving the problem?

The owner of a small corner shop has been facing increasing competition from the new Tesco Express that has opened at a petrol station nearby. It is offering a number of different products and the owner is keen to try and expand his stock to try and compete with them. Now a food safety inspector has forced him to buy a new fridge, to keep the cooked meats separate from the other chilled products.

The accountant has advised the shopkeeper to invest in a new IT system. It will monitor sales and costs more effectively than before. At the same time, the shopkeeper is working ever longer hours and wants to hire a part-time member of staff to try and give him a bit of a break. The problem is that he can't do all these things, so what does he do?

The government has been facing criticism about its response to antisocial behaviour in a number of inner-city housing estates. Young people have been hanging round the streets getting into trouble, causing a nuisance, setting cars on fire and breaking windows. The young people complain they have nothing else to do. The local residents are complaining that the police do not seem to be doing enough to combat the problems. 'There are never enough bobbies on the beat,' they argue.

The police know that there is a problem but say that they do not have the officers to be able to mount more patrols of these areas. They point out that they also have to police the city centre and that their resources are stretched.

Housing charities argue that the cause of many of the problems is the lack of respect for the area because of the run-down housing and the lack of facilities. Invest in improving these and the problems will diminish, they say. The government knows that more money put into these areas will have to come from somewhere. Should it spend less on something else or raise taxes? What should the government do?

Whatever choice we make, there is no right or wrong 'tag' that we can apply to it.

- If you chose to spend your £100 on an MP3 player, some people might say that was a good choice. Others might say that you have wasted your money and tell you that the sports equipment would have been a much better buy.
- The accountant might firmly believe the shopkeeper should have invested in the IT system rather than on the new cooler unit because it was more important to the overall success of the business.
- The government can never win – if they spend more on providing better facilities for young people they will be criticised for not supporting the police and local people by recruiting more officers.

It's all a matter of perspective, remember! However, what we can do is to look at the reasons why we made these choices. There may have been very good reasons why particular decisions have been made. An economist is interested in why decisions are made and what choices have been made – it tells us a great deal about the **value** we put on different things. We look at the concept of value in Unit 5.

Exercise

Consider the following issues:

- the decision by the government to ban smoking in July 2007 in pubs and clubs
- plans to charge motorists for using the road – possibly up to £1.30 per mile during peak times of the day when the roads are busiest
- plans to increase taxes on domestic flights (within the UK) to help combat carbon emissions.

For each issue, write a short paragraph explaining two opposing points of view. Remember that you must express your arguments in economic terms, not just general knowledge.

5 What is value?

This watch is worth £1,000.

In saying that, I have made a statement about the **value** of this watch.

Exercise

■ Do you agree with my statement? If so, why do you think it is 'worth' this amount of money?

■ If you disagree, what are your reasons?

If you disagree, you will probably be thinking along the lines of *'I would not spend £1,000 on that watch.'* You may think that you would not spend £1,000 on *any* watch, even if you had lots of money. You may think that you could do a lot of other things with the £1,000. Or that the watch does not appear to be of a sufficient quality to justify spending £1,000 on it.

If I told you that the watch is made out of platinum, the face contains polished diamond and hands are made from high quality white gold, would your view about the value of the watch change?

Value is another of the things that we often talk about without thinking. We use the concept every day in one form or another. We might not use the sort of terminology that an economist would use, but essentially we mean the same thing.

Each of the following statements is about value. Think about why.

1 I got this in the sale, it was a bargain!
2 What a waste of money that was.
3 I wish I had not gone to see that film, it was rubbish.
4 These jeans I bought are so cool.
5 I wouldn't swap it for anything.
6 The government have taken the decision to close down this RAF airfield because circumstances have changed significantly since it was first used in 1936.
7 Sending money to starving people is one thing but it's not what

they really need – what they need is practical help to sort out their own lives.

A dictionary definition of value sums it up as: *'An amount, expressed as goods, services, or money, considered to be a fair and suitable equivalent for something else.'*

When we talk about value we are expressing our opinion about what we would be prepared to exchange for a product or service.

Let's go back to the watch. I said that the value of the watch was £1,000. In this case, that is the value the seller puts on it. This means that we are being asked to exchange £1,000 in order to buy that watch.

We know that money is simply a means of exchange. I could use that same £1,000 to buy a range of other products and services. If I would rather use that £1,000 to buy something else, then the watch does not represent very good value to me. So if I say that I do not think it is 'worth' £1,000, I am saying that I would not be prepared to give up £1,000 (or what that £1,000 could buy me instead) in order to buy it.

So, money gives us a way to understand economic value. We can use this idea to look again at the list of statements.

1   I got this in the sale – it was a bargain.

> A 'bargain' is something we would have been prepared to pay more in order to obtain. We think it is worth more than we paid for it.

2   What a waste of money that was.

> The money we had to exchange could have been used to buy something else that we would much rather have had and that would have given us better value.

3   These jeans I bought are so cool.

> I spent quite a lot of amount of money on these jeans but the satisfaction they are giving me in terms of how I look and feel in them is well worth the money I have spent.

4   I wouldn't swap it for anything.

> There is nothing else that you can offer me that would have greater value for me than owning this particular item.

5   The government have taken the decision to close down this RAF airfield because circumstances have changed significantly since it was first used in 1936.

> When this airfield was first built it had a specific use. Now that the role of the RAF has changed, the airfield no longer fulfils the same function. We can use the money currently being spent on this airfield better somewhere else.

6 Sending money to starving people is one thing but it's not what they really need – what they need is practical help to sort out their own lives.

> The real value in helping people is to help them help themselves so that they do not have to rely on handouts. There is some value to sending them money but it is no substitute for practical things like tools or equipment to secure water supplies.

Value, like everything else we have looked at so far, means different things to different people, but at the heart of it is the notion of what we must exchange to buy the product or service.

We can link the concept of value to that of scarcity. Things tend to have a higher value the more scarce they are. In other words if the number of people wanting a product or service is much higher than the number that is available, then the value will be higher. This will be represented by the amount of money we are willing to give up to buy the product or service.

Exercise

1 We all know that diamonds are very 'valuable'. Explain why they are valuable, and how we know that.

2 Which of these two items is the most valuable to you:
- a ticket to see Brazil in training before a major football tournament?
- a mobile phone?

Explain your reasoning.

6 Satisfaction

You buy a product or service because you expect some satisfaction from consuming it. What is satisfaction and can we measure it? Finding an answer to this question is really important in economics because it helps us to understand a great deal about making choices. The problem is that different people have different levels of understanding about satisfaction.

Take this example. You have been playing sport for your school team. You have been running around for over an hour and the weather is warm and sunny – you are hot and thirsty. I have been standing on the sidelines enjoying the game and have got through two cans of lemonade during the game. The match finishes and you leave the field. One of your teachers comes up to you and offers you a bottle of orange juice; being generous, he also offers me one. Who will get the most satisfaction out of the drink – you or me?

Chances are that you think you will get the greater satisfaction. Indeed, that is likely to be the case. But does it mean that I will get no satisfaction at all from the drink? Not necessarily, it is just that you will get far more satisfaction than me. Exactly how much satisfaction is not easy to measure.

If we could place the measure of satisfaction on a scale of 1–10, what level of satisfaction would you give? Maybe 10/10? For me, having already drunk two cans of fizzy drink, the rating might be nearer 2/10.

You guzzle down the drink and the teacher offers you another carton – you thank him and take it. How much satisfaction will you get from this second carton of drink? More than likely, not as much as the first one – perhaps 8/10? If you are given a third carton, what level of satisfaction do you now get? Probably only 4 or 5/10.

What is all this to do with economics? Quite a lot. It is difficult to measure satisfaction, but we know that the more we consume of something the less additional satisfaction it gives us.

The satisfaction we gain from a product or service is a reflection of the value that we put on it. When you came off the pitch desperate for a drink, you may have placed a very high value on getting a drink because you were so thirsty.

In our example, the teacher gave you the drink for nothing. But what if he had asked you to pay for it? You might have been willing to give up (say) £2 to buy the drink at that moment in time. In economic terms, the value of the satisfaction gained from consuming a drink at that time was worth whatever £2 could also have bought you at that time. Your £2 might have been able to buy you some chocolate bars, crisps, fruit and so on but at that moment in time the drink gave you the greatest satisfaction.

The monetary value of something, therefore, is very closely linked to the satisfaction we think we will get from the consumption of that product.

Value in relation to income

I have just bought a CD for £12.99. It's music that I really like. For me, parting with £12.99 is a small price to pay. For one thing, £12.99 in comparison to my monthly income is a very small percentage. For another, I will listen to it over and over again so the amount of satisfaction I get from the consumption of this CD is worth much more to me than £12.99.

I could, of course, spend my £12.99 on other products. For example, I am quite partial to beer and £12.99 could buy me several cans. I would get satisfaction from drinking the beer over a period of time – possibly a week, but after that it is gone. The CD will still be there in years to come, enabling me to enjoy the music. So it is a small price to pay to buy a high level of satisfaction for me.

But how much would you pay for the same CD? For one thing, your musical tastes may be very different from mine. You may even hate the music I like, so you would not pay anything for the CD. I would not expect you, as a budding economist, to 'waste your money' on exchanging your hard-earned cash for something that gives you no satisfaction.

Say you have seen a CD that you would like for £10.49. It contains 14 tracks, compared to the 10 that are on my CD. Surely it represents better value for money? In some respects it might do, but not to me, because I prefer the music on my CD. I would not play your CD so it has no value to me – the album would give me little or no satisfaction.

Let us assume that you decide to buy the CD you want with money from your part-time job. This says something about the value you place on the album in comparison to the value I might place on my CD. Your level of income is likely to be much lower than mine. You might receive only £20 a week from a part-time job, yet choose to spend over half of that limited income on the CD. This reflects the level of value that you place on the CD.

Economists measure satisfaction not only by how much someone is spending, but also what proportion of their scarce resources this represents.

The exercise below pulls together the concepts of scarcity, choice, value and perspectives. When you are working through it, try to use the terms and concepts you have met so far in this book.

Exercise

1 **David Beckham spent a rumoured half a million pounds on a party for friends in May 2006.**

   Was this a wise use of scarce resources? Explain your answer.

2 **Ash Connor, a national council member of the Football Supporters' Federation said that the party was:** *'an obscene waste of money and that it would be better being given to grass roots football'.*

   Do you agree? Explain your answer.

3 **The party had many guests from the sporting and celebrity world including Robbie Williams, Elle McPherson and Freddie Flintoff. There were various charity auctions during the evening. Two tickets for members of the public to attend the party were auctioned before the event. That in itself raised over £100,000. All the proceeds from the money raised at the party went to different charities, including the National Society for the Prevention of Cruelty to Children (NSPCC).**

   Given this information, respond again to the opinion expressed by Ash Connor.

   David Beckham has funded The David Beckham Academy in London and Los Angeles where young people can experience the pleasure of playing football and also get expert coaching. The academy is open to players of all levels of ability.

Revision Essentials

Value is the worth of something represented by the amount of money we are prepared to give up to buy it.

Satisfaction is a personal measure of the fulfilment we feel from consuming a good or service.

7 Opportunity cost

Opportunity cost is one of the most important concepts running through the whole of the subject of economics. It is at the very heart of the way that economists think.

Let's review what we have said so far in Section 1.

Economics is all about **scarcity of resources** and **unlimited wants**. Because we have unlimited wants and needs but scarce resources, we have to make **choices** about how we spend our (scarce) money. When we make this choice we have in mind the **value** we place on things which we buy. This, in turn, is linked to the value we place on the other things that the money could also buy.

When we go to buy something, we know that we have a limited income – the money in our pockets. We know that we want to get more things than we can afford. We know as a result of this that we have to make a choice. And when we make a choice it means we are giving something up – the thing that we can't have.

Imagine that you have £10 and go to a music store to look for a CD. You see three CDs that you would like to buy but they are £9.99 each. You know that you cannot have all three and so have to decide which one to buy and which ones not to buy, In other words, you are giving up two of the three CDs.

How do you make your decision? You will have to weigh up a variety of things. You might you consider things like:

- whether you already have any other CDs by any of the artists you are considering buying
- how many tracks are on each CD or how long the CD plays for
- whether you will like all the tracks – you may have heard only one track on a CD and may not be sure whether you will like the rest
- the artwork and the album notes – one might be much more appealing than the others.

When you spend your money on one thing, you have to sacrifice what else that money could buy

There will be lots of things swirling through your mind when you are making your decision. You may not even be conscious of all these things but they will be there. Eventually, you settle on one choice and reluctantly put the other two back. To make your choice, you have had to sacrifice the other two CDs.

The economist would look at your decision and assume that you placed a higher value on the CD you chose than either of the other two. You go to the counter and pay for the CD. In handing over £9.99 you are saying to the shop, 'I value the satisfaction I will get from consuming this CD higher than anything else that this same £9.99 could have bought me at this time.'

What we have looked at here is the mechanics of making choices. Whatever choice we make we have to make a sacrifice and what we sacrifice says far more about our decision than quoting an amount of money.

In economics, every decision by every individual, business, government and international institution is part of a complex web of signals that demonstrates our view about value and satisfaction. The cost to us of something is not the money we have to give up but what we sacrifice when we make a choice. Looking at the sacrifice gives us far more information about scarcity, choice and the allocation of those scarce resources than simply seeing how much money we have spent. This is what opportunity cost is all about.

> **Revision Essentials**
> **Opportunity cost** is the cost expressed in terms of the next best alternative that has been given up.

When economists look at how much the government has spent on the **NHS**, they are less concerned about the money, and more about what has been sacrificed in making that choice. As a result of the money spent on the NHS, perhaps less has been available to spend on education, or on policing the streets.

Next we look at three examples of opportunity costs.

Opportunity cost to business

A business is contemplating attempting to boost its sales revenue and is looking at two possible approaches. One is a promotional campaign aimed at specific target markets, which has been informed by information it has received from recent market research. The second is a new advertising campaign that would be planned and developed by an external advertising agency with a reputation for results. Its budget is such that it cannot do both and must choose between one of the strategies. It chooses to go with the promotional campaign. The opportunity cost is the advertising campaign it has to sacrifice.

Opportunity cost to the government

Some patients in the early stages of breast cancer have put pressure on the government and their local National Health Service (NHS) trusts to prescribe a new drug, Herceptin, as part of their treatment. The cost to the NHS of treating one patient with Herceptin is over £21,000 for a year of treatment. Local hospitals argue that the increase in their costs to use the drug would be significant and might affect other patients. The cost of a hip replacement, for example, is around £4,000. In this case, the opportunity cost of treating one patient with Herceptin would

be about five patients who might not receive their hip replacements that year.

Opportunity cost to international organisations

A major international charity is working in a less developed country, dealing with famine victims. It has received significant sums in donations from the public and must now decide how to allocate these funds. It can channel the money into immediate relief efforts aimed at providing basic foodstuffs to the victims. It knows that if it does this the long-term situation will not improve and the problem might simply re-occur in future years. An alternative would be to put the funds into providing tools and equipment that would help the people to manage their own affairs more effectively and provide food for themselves in the longer term. They decide to go for this solution, the opportunity cost is several thousand people who may die in the next three months through a lack of food.

These three examples are quite stark. In reality, not every decision is a straight either/or situation. However, many choices are tough ones. The principle of opportunity cost is so important to economics that you should always keep it in mind. The units that follow are designed to encourage you to do this.

Exercise

1   Choose one of the three situations described above. Which choice would you have made, and why? Remember that you are being asked to make a judgement here. It must be supported with some sound reasoning. Do some research into the issues to help you get the evidence to support your answer.

8 Price

'I bought a Coke and it cost me 65p.' A simple statement, the sort of thing that many of us have said hundreds of times. However, there is one flaw in the statement. It did not **cost** the person 65p – what they mean is that the **price** they had to pay to buy the item was 65p. In economics, the 'cost' of a Coke refers to the sum of the **inputs** that the manufacturers had to pay out to produce the item. These inputs are classified as land, labour, capital and enterprise.

Many people make the mistake of confusing 'price' and 'cost'. In this unit we will be thinking about the price we have to pay to buy a product or service.

Let's look in a bit more detail about the notion of price and cost. What is a bottle of Coke? It is the result of a massive production operation that involves the use of land, labour, machinery and equipment (capital) and some element of risk being taken (enterprise) by those who organise the production of Coke. The 65p you are being asked to pay to buy a bottle of Coke represents slices of the payments the firm has to make for each of these so-called **'factors of production'**. It might divide up as follows:

- land – 8p
- labour – 20p
- capital – 35p
- enterprise – 2p.

These costs are what the producer has to account for. In setting a price, they will have to bear in mind that they must cover their costs and they will also want to make some element of profit (the reward for their enterprise). They could, of course, charge 70p per bottle and look to make 7p profit. But they must also have in mind what they think their customers will believe is a reasonable price to pay.

For buyers the situation is different. If I go into a food store, I am faced with an array of bottled drinks. I can buy a bottle of Coke or choose from a wide range of other soft drinks. We have already seen that in making choices we are weighing up the satisfaction we will gain from one product as opposed to another. In this case, I scan the shelves and focus on two items – a bottle of **Coke** and a bottle of **Sprite**.

Two drinks – slightly different taste, similar prices. How do I make my decision which one to buy?

I also know that if I choose the bottle of Sprite, the opportunity cost will be the bottle of Coke that I have sacrificed. If both bottles are priced at 65p, then my decision might be based on which I prefer at that moment in time. If the bottle of Sprite is priced at 75p then I might have more complicated factors affecting my decision. Is the extra 10p I am being asked to pay for the Sprite worth it? Will I get an extra 10p's worth of satisfaction from that bottle of Sprite? I might decide that 10p is neither here nor there and go for the Sprite, but if the difference was 20p I might think again. After all, they are both fizzy drinks, I am thirsty, yes, but both will quench my thirst and the difference in the taste is not that wide.

The drink that I eventually choose to buy will be a reflection of all those things, but ultimately I am being asked to give up a sum of money to buy that drink. That sum of money could have bought me other things and so it is also a statement of the value I attach to that drink over what else my money could buy at that time.

Economics has a number of theories that are linked to an assumption that human beings behave rationally. This means that humans behave consistently – that they would do the same thing over and over if they had the same choice.

If choosing the bottle of Coke gives me a satisfaction rating of 9/10 and a bottle of Sprite 7/10, then it makes sense for me to buy the bottle of Coke. Handing over my 65p gives me a greater return when buying the Coke than it does with the Sprite. This is what **rational** behaviour is all about.

Prices therefore act as a signal to both consumers and producers. To producers, the price they are able to charge is a reflection of the costs of production. It also includes an element of reward for the risk they are taking in producing that product or service. It lets a producer know whether, to them, it is worth making the product or service.

For the consumer, price acts as a signal telling us whether the sacrifice we are making in giving up the opportunity to buy other goods is worth it. It gives us a way of measuring the degree of satisfaction that we get from a product.

SALE
Up to 75% off!

Stores will try and persuade us to part with our money by reducing prices. When prices are reduced like this it changes the relationship between the value of other things we might want to buy and our notion of value

Revision Essentials

Price: the amount of money we are asked to give up to buy a good or service.

Cost: the amount a producer has to pay to produce a good or service.

Factors of production: a classification of the four main things needed to produce any good or service. These are:

- land (all the natural resources of the earth
- labour (all the mental and physical human effort that goes towards production)
- capital (machinery and equipment that is used to help production)
- enterprise (the risk taken in organising the other factors to produce products and services).

Inputs: everything that goes into the production process, e.g. the ingredients and labour.

Rational: being logical and consistent when making choices.

When prices rise or fall they send powerful messages to both producers and consumers that change our behaviour. This is the subject of the next unit – markets.

Investigation

Conduct a survey of family and friends to find out satisfaction levels in consumption.

- Select four brands of products of your choice – they could be anything from soft drinks to washing tablets – and note the prices.
- Ask respondents to rate their satisfaction with the products on a scale of 1–10, with 10 being maximum satisfaction.
- Ask your respondents to name one alternative product they would buy instead of each of the ones you have chosen and get them to rate the satisfaction level of the substitute products. Find out the the prices of the alternative products.
- Analyse your results and discuss what they tell you about the relationship between price and the value people place on consumption.

9 Markets

A market is any place that brings together buyers and sellers with a view to agreeing a price. The market stall is a traditional form of market, but there are many others including shops and Internet sites. There are markets everywhere, with sellers offering goods and services and us, the consumer, deciding whether or not we want to buy.

When you go into a supermarket, the store is offering thousands of different products for sale. The prices will be clearly stated. You browse round the store and make dozens of choices before going to the checkout. Every time you make a decision you are sending a signal to producers. They are learning about the value you place on their products in relation to the price they are asking you to pay.

For example, when buying washing tablets for the laundry, your parents must choose from dozens of different brands and products. Each manufacturer is trying to tempt buyers to choose their brand instead of a rival. Their strategies might include the attractiveness of the packaging, the ease of use, the price, and the effects on the environment.

Products in a store – all vying to grab your attention!

When they make a choice, for example **Persil**, your parents are saying to manufacturer: 'We think that the price you are asking for this item reflects the value that we'll get from the product.' They are also saying to every other manufacturer of washing tablets: 'We don't think the value represented by your product and the price you are asking us to pay in return for that product is worth it at this time.'

You might think that individuals' spending decisions do not make much difference. Remember, though, that you are one of millions of people making decisions every day. Together, the consumer has a great deal of power and markets work because of the effectiveness of price as a signal.

Imagine that the sales of a particular washing tablets (Brand A) are doing very well indeed. One of their rivals, on the other hand, Brand B is not doing at all well. Its sales are falling. The message to the manufacturers of Brand B is that there is something not quite right about the product. It might be the cleaning power of the tablets, dull packaging or the price being charged – or a combination of these factors. For the consumer the price just does not represent value for money compared to the price they are being asked to pay for Brand A.

The manufacturers of Brand B must do something about this. They could decide to stop manufacturing altogether or they could:

- look to see if they can do something about the price
- make production more efficient to lower their production costs (which would allow them to be able to do something with the price)
- change the formulation of the product, the packaging and so on.

Meanwhile, managers of Brand A can see from the level of sales that their product represents good value for money as far as the consumer is concerned. They have clearly got things right – at the moment. They might even take the opportunity of pushing up the price by a few pence to increase the element of profit they are getting from each packet. They think that the customer will accept this because of the strength of sales.

However, in the meantime, Brand B has done some work. The manufacturers have made a number of changes and a year later launch a new improved Brand B into stores. It is backed by a massive campaign to promote the product – to ensure customers know about it. Six months after the launch, it seems that the efforts have worked. Brand B sales have increased.

For Brand A, the story is a bit different. Since Brand B was re-launched they have noticed sales gradually falling back. It now seems that customers prefer Brand B to Brand A! The manufacturers of Brand A are being sent a different message by customers' buying behaviour: 'I used to think your product represented better value for money but now I am getting more satisfaction from exchanging my money for Brand B rather than your product.' Brand A managers have to respond – they might do something with the price, the packaging…and so on.

Brand A and Brand B are just two of the products that are in competition with each other. All manufacturers know that consumers have a choice. So they have to identify, anticipate and meet customer needs to persuade them to choose their product over any other that might be available.

This is how markets work – a constant battle between producers in competition with each other. Most are focused on the consumers, to persuade them to part with their money. As consumers, we are constantly being asked to make choices. Sometimes the range of goods on offer is so wide that choosing is difficult. Fortunately, price acts as a signal to help us make that choice.

So, markets consist of buyers and sellers. Buyers represent the demand for a product and sellers represent the supply of a product. When buyers and sellers come together you have a market. Price is the common signal that enables both producers and consumers to make decisions.

A street market – bringing together buyers and sellers

Shortages

If a good or service is very popular for some reason, then there will be more buyers than sellers willing or able to offer it for sale. In these circumstances there will be a shortage in the market and sellers will see the opportunity to push prices up. As the price rises, some of those customers might decide that it no longer represents value for money and drop out of the market.

For producers, a rising price is a signal that there are customers out there willing to pay for that product or service. As a result, it is worth their while trying to supply the product or service. As price continues to rise, more consumers drop out and more producers try to increase supply. While the shortage exists, prices will stay high, but once the shortage disappears prices should slip back to their original level.

Surpluses

The opposite can also occur. If there are more sellers offering a product or service than there are buyers who want to buy it then there will be a surplus. The pressure on price in this case will be to fall. As price falls, some consumers who previously might have thought the price too high now enter the market. For producers, some will now be at the stage where their costs are higher than the price they are receiving, so they drop out of the market. As this process continues, the surplus gradually disappears.

We can see this market process happening all the time. Markets are dynamic – they are constantly changing. The process can take years to occur in some cases, but in others the process might be more immediate. There is a tendency to think that all these changes happen instantaneously. They do not.

Prices, we have said, act as signals. They act as signals to influence behaviour. Sometimes that behaviour can change quickly but in other cases it might take many months or even years. Producers, for example, might be faced with falling prices but they might have built huge, expensive factories and cannot easily afford to cut back these production levels.

Equally, consumer behaviour takes time to adjust. For example, cigarette prices have increased a great deal in recent years – mostly as a result of the tax that governments have put on them. This has persuaded some people to give up smoking. For many others, their behaviour has not changed – they still smoke because of the addictive nature of cigarettes. So we have to look at many factors when analysing markets (i.e. when we are breaking down what is happening to enable us to understand the process more easily).

Exercise

1 In early 2006, there were reports of a dead swan in northern Scotland. Tests on the bird discovered that it was the more serious strain of avian flu (bird flu) that had killed the bird. At the time of the news, the average price of a chicken in supermarkets was around £3.75. Poultry farmers around the UK had feared this moment for some time. In parts of Asia, a number of humans had died from contracting the virus that causes avian flu. Was this going to be another food scare?

   ■ Describe what you think might happen to the market for chicken as a result of this scenario. Remember to consider what might happen to producers (in this case, the producers are the farmers and the supermarkets) and also what the response of consumers might be. Your answer should explain what you think will happen to the price and also the amount of chickens bought and sold. Remember also the importance of time in determining how both producers and consumers respond to changing circumstances.

2 The summer of 2006 started off quite cold. May was rainy and temperatures were below average. Companies providing packaged holidays abroad rubbed their hands – they had holidays to sell in countries where the sun could be almost guaranteed! However, there was only a certain number of seats on the planes and a certain number of rooms in the hotels around resorts in Europe that they had available. The weather in June in the UK was no better.

   ■ Explain what you think might happen to the market for packaged holidays as a result of the situation above. Make sure that you explain the response of both consumers and producers to the scenario and what you think will happen to the price and the number of packaged holidays that are bought and sold.

10 Market failure

We have said that markets use prices to send signals to both consumers and producers. The market is working well if those prices do two things:

- provide the customer with value for money when purchasing something
- cover the costs of production and therefore provide enough income to producers

The signals that we get from prices influence our behaviour. If the signal does not work very well for some reason, our behaviour will be different and we may not necessarily be happy with the results.

Markets need to have excellent sources of information to work effectively. Where prices do not act as appropriate signals, markets will not work as well and there will be what is called '**market failure**'.

Market failure results in shortages or surpluses of things continuing to exist. For example, there is never enough affordable housing for young people in London. This lack of supply is a market failure. Why should this occur when our understanding of the market so far would suggest that shortages and surpluses would disappear after a period of time?

If there are surpluses, it means that consumers do not want to buy goods and services at the prices being asked, and if there are shortages it means that they would like to buy more of the particular product or service. Either way, this is an inefficient use of resources and leads to either underproduction or overproduction – shortages and surpluses that do not go away!

In these cases, price is not acting as an appropriate signal. This can be for a variety of reasons. One of the main reasons is that many products and services are taxed, with the result that consumers find it difficult to understand exactly what the price really represents.

Take petrol, for example. Say that the average price of a litre of petrol is 95p. Of that amount, 47.1p is the duty levied on petrol by the government. So 95p per litre is not the 'true' price (i.e. the price that reflects the costs of production and the element of profit that a business requires for producing products).

Market failure also occurs when we do not know exactly what we are buying. For example, if **Daz** tell us that their product is 'new and improved' and that it washes better than other soap powders, how do we know for sure that what they are telling us is correct? If we are being asked to pay £80 for a pair of **Nike** trainers and £20 for a pair of non-branded trainers, how do we know that the Nike trainers are four times the quality or value of the non-branded pair? The short answer is that we do not. That means that firms can try to persuade us to part with our money in all sorts of different ways and it is more difficult for us, as consumers, to get an accurate signal from the price being asked.

We see market failure occurring in other cases that are very familiar to us:

- Congestion on roads – caused by drivers not paying the true cost of motoring.
- Testing of products on animals – how do we know which products have been tested on animals and which have not?
- What products contain – do we really know what is in that **McDonalds** Big Mac?
- Pollution – caused by businesses and so on, not taking into account the true cost of production.
- Unemployment – caused by people not having the necessary skills for jobs in their area; by people not being able to move to where jobs might be available; or by discrimination.
- High prices and less choice – caused by some firms being in a position where they can exert control on the market.
- Poverty – caused by an inability of some people or areas to access the sort of resources they need to be able to improve their position.
- Non-provision of some goods and services – caused by the fact that it is almost impossible to charge a price for some products or services (for example, 'defence' and 'justice').
- Over-use of non-renewable resources – over-fishing, using too many natural resources like oil and gas, caused by the fact that it is sometimes difficult to establish who owns what. For example, who owns the sea, from which fish are being extracted to the point where some species might end up becoming extinct?
- Over-production of some goods that are not 'good', for example, gambling, non-medicinal drugs, cigarettes and alcohol.

We will deal with all these issues and others in later sections. Remember that many of the problems we face in economics are simply down to the fact that markets are not working properly. Suggesting solutions to combat market failure is relatively easy. However, putting these solutions into practice is not quite so simple, because it affects so many people in different ways. That is why we have so many different perspectives on similar issues.

Investigation

Part of the assessment for this module is to produce an investigation. We can make a start by looking at some of the things we have covered in this first introductory section.

Choose *one* of the topics below and carry out some research to find out more.

1 Successive dry winters in the south-east of England have left water levels very low. Water companies have predicted that there might be shortages in the summer months, especially if the weather is hot and dry. Some companies have imposed restrictions on the use of water. In the north, they have no such problems – they have plenty of water!

Dry winters mean people in the south-east have water shortages

a) Discuss the likely success of three different solutions to the water shortage problem.

b) To what extent is limiting the use of water the solution to the shortages in the south-east?

2 In the past two years, oil prices have risen significantly. Oil companies claim that there are plenty of supplies available but this does not seem to have had any effect on the price which has continued to rise.

a) What is the major cause of the rise in oil prices in the last two years?

b) What is the most important impact of the rise in oil prices on the UK economy?

3 An auction in May 2006 was held to sell off a painting by the artist Picasso. The winning bidder paid over £52 million for the painting.

a) Assess the importance of opportunity cost to this particular scenario.

b) To what extent do you think that the winning bidder received 'value for money' as a result of winning the auction?

A waste of money or a bargain?

SECTION 2

RISK OR CERTAINTY?

What is meant by success in business?

Judging business success

Think about a business that you consider to be successful. What do you think makes the business successful? Is it the size? How about the amount of money or profit they make? Maybe it's because people like their image? These things are all important to business success.

There are ways of checking how well a business is doing. Economists measure business success in two ways:

1 **quantitative measures** – this refers to things that we can measure by quantity, like profit
2 **qualitative measures** – these are used for things like the firm's image and reputation and are more difficult to measure accurately.

In this unit, we look at quantitative measures. We will look at qualitative measures in Unit 12.

Quantitative measures

Here we look at things that can be measured by quantity.

Profit

Profit is the difference between the amount of revenue earned by a firm and the total costs of producing the goods and services the business sells. We can write this in a simple formula:

Profit = Total Revenue – Total Cost

Revenue

The revenue of a business is calculated by multiplying the number of goods or services sold by the price at which they are sold. The formula, therefore, is:

Revenue = Quantity x Price

For example, if an ice cream seller sells 150 Magnum ice creams in a week at a price of £1.10 each, the weekly revenue would be £165.

Many businesses do not only sell one product or service. They sell different items at different prices. The principle is the same, however.

The easiest way for a shop to work out its revenue is to add up all the cash and credit sales recorded at the till.

Selling goods and services is obviously vital to a business's success. Yet some businesses do very nicely by selling small quantities, but at very high prices, for example, **Vertu** mobile phones that sell for as much as £100,000 each (they are diamond-encrusted). Other businesses sell very large quantities but at low prices.

Exercise

Identify six different businesses, three which sell only a small amount of goods at high prices and three which are volume sellers (i.e. they sell very large amounts at relatively low prices).

Costs

Before we can judge whether a firm is successful or not in terms of its turnover, we have to investigate what its costs are like. Costs refer to all the payments that a business has to make to produce the good or service and get it to their customers. These costs will be varied and depend to a large extent on the type of business.

We classify costs in two main ways – fixed costs (or 'overheads') and variable costs. **Fixed costs** are costs that do not depend on the amount of output produced. Fixed costs have to be paid regardless of whether the business sells anything that it has produced. They are fixed in relation to output. However, this does not mean they never change – they do.

Examples of fixed costs include things like business rates – a tax that has to be paid to a local council, administration costs such as postage, rent, insurance, advertising costs and many more. These costs have to be paid whether the business sells anything or not. They do change though – for example, insurance costs can rise, and interest charges can rise or fall.

There are other costs that vary directly with the amount produced. These are called **variable costs**. They rise if the amount produced (output) rises and fall if output falls. The most obvious example of variable costs are raw materials and component parts – things like the chips used in computers, the tyres used in producing a car and the batteries that come with a mobile phone.

If, for example, **Nokia** produces an extra 20,000 mobiles each week, it will have to pay for an extra 20,000 batteries to go with the phones, so the variable costs of production will also rise.

There are some costs that are difficult to place in these two categories. Costs like wages, for example – is a wage a fixed cost or a variable cost? The answer is that it depends. If a worker on an hourly wage is asked to work an extra 10 hours a week, then the cost of employing that worker will rise with the amount of work done. In this case, we would classify the cost as a variable cost. Some people work for a salary. Your teacher is most likely to be on an annual salary – let us assume that it is £25,000 a year. Whether they work 18 hours a day or 8, they will still get the same amount of money at the end of each month. In this case, the cost of labour would be classed as a fixed cost.

Costs of production

We can put the two classifications of costs together to get the total costs of production. The formula for total costs is:

Total Costs = Variable Costs plus Fixed Costs

If we compare revenue and costs we can see where profit comes from. It is important to make sure that you understand the difference between the revenue that is generated from selling goods or services and profit – they are not the same thing.

We might say a firm is successful if it is 'making money' but we need to be careful about what we mean by 'making money'. Some firms generate huge revenues from sales – they could be classed as 'making money'. Firms such as **Vodafone** have a very high turnover (another word for revenue) but if you then take into account their costs, then the actual profit they make might not be very much, or even becomes a loss.

A loss occurs when the total costs are greater than the total revenue. Just because a firm makes a loss does not mean it is going to close down, but it is a signal to the business to do something to either change its costs or its revenues. Few firms can suffer making losses for a long time.

In June 2006, Vodafone announced that it had revenues for the year standing at £29.3 billion – that's £29,300,000,000! You might think that this would make the company successful, and in many ways Vodafone is a successful company. However, when it took into account the costs of running the business and also having to reduce the value of the assets that it owned (assets represent the value of a company's buildings, equipment, machinery, stock and so on) the business made a loss of £23.5 billion – the biggest company loss in the history of European business.

When a business is the size of Vodafone, the classification of its costs and its revenues becomes very complex. The announcement of the loss looked bad, but if you looked at the figures more closely, the costs involved were high because the business had to revalue some of its assets. It actually did very well in terms of the amount of services it sold and the cost of providing those services.

12 Measures of success in business

As we saw at the end of Unit 11, judging a firm by its profit (or loss) needs a bit of care. To help make more sense of the quantitative measure of a business's success, we need to put several pieces of information together. It is usually helpful to make comparisons between different types of information, e.g. finding out how much profit has been made per £ of sales.

Gross profit margin

Profit margin is the percentage difference between the revenue and the cost of the product. You will hear of business people talking about 'narrow' or 'squeezed' margins. This means that the difference between the selling price and the cost is getting smaller. If a seller of fish and chips charges £4 for a portion of cod and chips and the cost of supplying that portion is £3.60, the seller is making 40p profit out of every £4 spent (i.e. a 10 per cent profit margin). If a rival chip shop had costs of £2.80 for its £4 meal, its profit margin would be £1.20 out of £4, (i.e. 30 per cent).

Profit margins are also expressed as percentages. If you bought a CD for £8.00 but sold it to a friend for £10.00, you would make a profit of £2.00. This represents a 20 per cent profit margin. Profit margins can be found by this formula:

$$\textbf{Profit Margin} = \frac{\textbf{Profit}}{\textbf{Revenue}} \textbf{ X 100}$$

Businesses focus upon two profit margin figures: the gross margin and the net margin.

Gross profit is the difference between the total revenue and the total variable costs: the actual costs of producing the goods. For example, take the manufacture of packets of crisps. The total variable costs include the costs of potatoes, the oil used to fry them, flavourings, packaging and the labour used in the manufacture. This figure does not include all the administration costs, the cost of advertising, insurance and so on. So, gross profit margin is:

$$\text{Gross Profit Margin} = \frac{\text{Gross Profit}}{\text{Revenue}} \times 100$$

Net profit margin

Net profit measures profit when both the variable and the fixed costs (overheads) are taken away from revenue.

$$\text{Net Profit Margin} = \frac{\text{Net profit}}{\text{Revenue}} \times 100$$

Here are some examples of the net margins earned by companies: **Tesco** operates with net margins of 6 per cent, i.e. it makes 6p profit out of every £ spent at the cash tills. **Sainsbury's** has net margins of less than 3 per cent, i.e. it makes less than half the profit per £ achieved by its great rival Tesco.

Qualitative measures of success

Assuming that the figures we are working with are accurate and reliable, there is not much dispute about quantitative measures of success. But with qualitative measures of success, how well or badly a firm is doing is more a matter of opinion.

Think about this question. Is **Prada** a successful business? What do you associate with this brand?

A Prada bag carrying the brand name

If you said things like quality, design, expensive prices, exclusivity and celebrities, the company would be pleased, because this is how it wants the Prada brand to be perceived. To survive, a business does need to make a profit, but business success often means more than this, which is where qualitative measures come in. Qualitative issues include:

- long-term survival
- image and reputation
- environmental awareness
- ethical responsibilities
- brand awareness.

Long-term survival

Many new businesses might enjoy some success in the first few years of their existence. In many cases, this does not mean that the business will survive in the longer term. Planning for long-term survival might mean sacrificing short-term profit for longer-term survival. Think about it this way: would you rather make £100,000 a year for five years but then see the business have to close a year or two later, or achieve a profit level of £50,000 for five years but have the business survive for another 20 years after that?

We can see two important economic concepts at work here – **opportunity cost** and **trade-offs**. A trade-off is a situation where a decision has to be made and in doing so, some form of sacrifice has to be made to achieve a longer-term gain.

Exercise

A small private limited company has had a successful first year and has generated profits of £100,000. Things are looking promising and sales have been strong. The shareholders of the business are three friends. They have a meeting to plan for the future.

- One is arguing that they have put in a huge amount of work and ought to take the profit and start to enjoy themselves.
- The second suggests that this is just the start of the hard work and if they want to ensure the future survival of the business they need to put back most of the profit into the business and buy new equipment and machinery to help the business improve.
- The third takes the middle ground, suggesting that they take some of the profit for themselves and put back the rest into the business.

1 What is the trade-off that the three shareholders have got to decide on?
2 What is the opportunity cost of each of the first two options?

Image and reputation

Business success is influenced by the image or reputation that a firm has managed to build up – sometimes over a long period of time. Having an image of being cool, trendy, trustworthy or reliable can add value to a firm's brand name. In 2007, **Toyota** overtook Ford to become the second-biggest-selling car brand in America (the biggest is General Motors). This occurred because Americans trusted the Japanese firm to produce more fuel-efficient and environmentally-friendly cars.

These things do not just happen. Businesses have to work hard and often spend large amounts of money over a long period of time to get to this stage. Many years of hard work can be damaged in just a short period of time. For example, oil producer **BP** has been affected by a series of incidents that led to an explosion in an oil refinery in Texas in which 15 people died. This, plus a serious oil spill in Alaska, suddenly hit BP's reputation in its largest single market: America.

Environmental awareness

In November 2006, Sir Nicholas Stern, a respected economist, published a report called *The Economics of Climate Change*. The report presented a vivid picture of the potential economic damage that climate change could cause. Many businesses have become more aware of the importance that their stakeholders now place on environmental issues. Many firms are looking at the effect that their activity is having on the environment.

The major supermarkets, for example, have been trying to convince us that they are finding ways of reducing the impact of the number of shopping bags that we use. Every year 1.7 billion bags are used in Sainsbury's stores alone and most of them do not rot down (they are not biodegradable). A similar problem occurs with the number of nappies used.

Many larger firms now produce a yearly report giving details of the costs of their activities on the environment. They also explain the measures that they are taking to try and reduce those costs. This might include switching to more fuel-efficient cars or vans, installing energy-saving devices in factories and offices, or reducing packaging and the levels of harmful emissions and waste.

These businesses wish to show their customers that they take their environmental responsibilities seriously. However, this might be a ploy to try to boost sales and retain customer loyalty rather than a genuine concern for the environment. An investigation into this issue would make an interesting piece of coursework.

Ethical responsibilities

Many people would now equate business success not just with profit but also with how the business behaves – its ethical responsibilities. We will look at this in more detail in Unit 27.

Brand awareness

Researchers have conducted an experiment to see if people could tell the difference between **Coca-Cola** and **Pepsi**. They used a brain scanner to find out more about how we think about and recognise different products and brands.

When people were given the two drinks, but were not told what they were drinking, they chose on a 50:50 basis. The experiment was repeated, but this time the people were told that one was Coca-Cola. This time, the choice was 70:30 in favour of Coca-Cola.

The brain-scanning technology recorded what was happening to the brain when the people were given this information and during the test. They came to the conclusion that the lifetime exposure to the advertising of a brand like Coca-Cola has a big impact on how we make choices of what to buy. Lots of advertising of a brand can, over a long time, make a significant difference to our choices.

This experiment highlights the importance that firms place on brand awareness. They want you, as a potential customer, to associate their brand with something recognisable and distinctive. That, they hope, will influence your choices when you spend your money. Raising brand awareness can lead to a higher chance of customers coming back time after time to buy a product – known as **repeat purchasing**. It is about persuading you to select a particular product from lots of other similar ones, for example, getting you to choose a **Mars** bar from the display of lots of other chocolate bars when you go into a store.

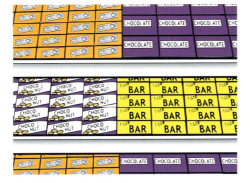

Investigation

Select one business that you are familiar with.

1 Choose three from the four main qualitative factors outlined in this section that you think contribute to the success of the business you have chosen.

2 Which of the three factors that you have identified do you think is the most important in their success? Explain your reasoning.

Investigation

Choose one business that you think is successful. This could be a local business or a well-known major national or international business.

1 Identify four reasons why you think that the business is successful – select a mixture of qualitative and quantitative factors.

2 Offer an explanation of each of the four reasons that you have identified (about 200 words per reason). Make sure that you relate the reasons specifically to the business you have chosen.

3 Given your explanation, which of the reasons you have identified do you think is the most important? Explain your reasoning.

13 Why do some businesses fail to survive?

Introduction to why businesses fail

Business failure occurs for one of two reasons:

1 The firm's cash flow is so weak that it can no longer pay its staff or suppliers.
2 The revenue earned by the firm from selling its products is not sufficient to cover its costs.

Many firms make losses at some point in their history but this does not mean that they will inevitably close down. In the long run, however, they do have to make a profit to survive. If they continue to make losses and are unable to do anything about turning the situation around, they will eventually have to cease production.

When a business gets to the stage where they are not able to carry on trading, they face a number of options:

- They can simply close the business and cease trading. Depending on the type of business organisation, the people who are owed money may or may not get what they are owed.
- In some cases, a business in trouble may be taken over by another business and changes made to improve it.
- In other cases, a business may get to the stage where it calls in someone to help it. This is generally a firm of accountants called 'administrators' or 'receivers'. These firms specialise in trying to find ways of solving the business's problems. If the business is to close, the administrators will try to sell off whatever assets the firm has left and pay off as many creditors (people and organisations who are owed money) as possible. If it is possible that the business could continue in some form, the administrators may try to find other firms to buy it.

The **MG Rover** company had to close in April 2005 because it was making big losses. A firm of administrators spent over a year looking to try and sort out the problems and find other businesses that might be interested in buying it. Eventually, a Chinese firm, Nanjing Engineering, bought some of the Rover business. Plans are ongoing to try and get some form of car production going again at the Longbridge plant.

In many cases, if a rescue plan is possible, the firm that comes out of the end of the process looks very different from the original, for example, it often has far fewer staff.

Challenges that businesses face

Modern businesses face many challenges and changes in circumstances. If a firm does not do anything about them, or if the things they try to remedy the situation do not work, then ultimately they can to lead to the closure of the business. In economics we call this 'exit from the industry/market'.

Changes in demand

Demand represents customers; if the number of customers falls, then a firm is likely to receive lower revenues. If its revenue falls but the costs of production do not fall by a greater amount, then the firm's profits will fall. If demand continues to fall and the firm cannot reduce its costs then eventually it will start to make losses. If these continue, then the firm may have to exit the market.

Changes in demand can be caused by a variety of reasons:

- changing fashions
- changes to the amount of money that people have available to spend (e.g. when interest rates rise and therefore mortgages take up more of the household budget)
- changes in the price of substitutes, (i.e. other products or services that can be used instead)
- changes in the price of complements (i.e. products that tend to be bought together, such as DVD players and DVDs)
- changes in the size and structure of the population – for example, the UK has an increasing number of people over 65 in the population, who tend to have different wants and needs from those of younger people
- expectations of consumers – rumours about food safety, for example, can lead to some consumers deciding not to buy certain types of foods
- advertising campaigns by rival firms.

The economy

The economy is an important factor that affects the success and failure of a business. Its influence occurs through many different ways and through a huge range of inter-connected effects. We will look in more detail at the economy in Unit 14.

Changes in technology

The rate at which technology is changing is rapid. If a firm is not able to keep up with these changes and meet customer needs then it might find itself in trouble.

Companies in the music industry have faced huge challenges from the growth of computer technology and the Internet. The developments in broadband technology and the widespread availability of PCs and MP3 players might see CDs disappear (in the same way that cassettes are now not often used). In a survey in 2006, a group of young people were asked whether they thought CDs would still be around in five years' time. Sixty per cent of them thought that they would not. The challenge for the music industry is to adjust to the different ways in which people are now choosing to access their music.

Failure to control costs

A teacher took a group of students to visit a factory that made computer chips. The owner of the factory stopped at one point and picked up a small computer chip off the floor. 'That's £5 saved,' he said. The point he was making was that everything a business does involves a cost of some kind. It might be buying raw masterials, employing labour, providing a staff canteen and uniform, paying for gas, heating, electricity, telephones, stamps, envelopes, coffee, water machines and so on.

If a business does not keep a close watch on these costs they can start to rise, with the result that the business becomes inefficient (i.e. it is not producing at the lowest possible cost). If costs rise and are not controlled then profit levels will be affected. The firm might eventually be squeezed out by competitors.

Cash-flow problems

Firms must ensure that they have enough cash to pay their bills. This sounds easy, but can be difficult, for example:

- a seaside hotel needing to redecorate in the winter
- a firework producer struggling through the spring months
- a small cake producer, suffering when a supermarket disputes a bill and refuses to pay.

Cash is the lifeblood of business. Banks happily offer loans to firms that

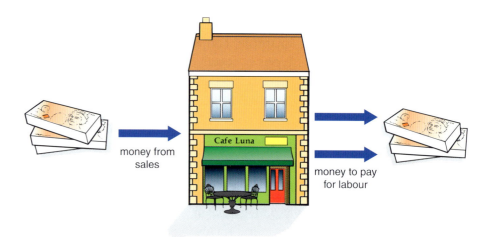

money from sales

money to pay for labour

control cash flow efficiently, but are hard on those with poor cash-flow management.

This problem affects large and small firms. Small and new firms, however, are particularly vulnerable. If bills are due to be paid and a firm does not have the cash available, it might end up in court.

In many cases, firms that have had to close down because of cash-flow problems have a perfectly good business model, but are simply unable to get the cash they are owed to be paid at the time they need it. More businesses fail because of cash-flow problems than any other single reason.

Poor management

Managing a business means looking after all the resources that go into production and sales. Getting the management right is a skill that does not come easily to everyone. Some people in management positions may confuse their own importance with the aims and focus of the business. They may be disorganised or not strong enough to make difficult decisions when they need to be made. When this happens, the business can start to suffer and can eventually fail.

A business consultant was invited into a medium-sized business to help out with the problems it was having. He soon spotted that costs were out of control. His first piece of advice came as a shock to the managers of the business. The consultant looked out into the car park. 'Why do you need to have five top-of-the-range BMWs to drive around in? Get rid of them and if you really need a company car, get something smaller, like a Ford Fiesta!' By doing this, the company cut costs by £220,000 in one go.

Growth of competition

Growth in competition might be a factor that contributes to a fall in demand. However successful a firm is, it needs to keep a close watch on the activities of new entrants into the industry.

The music industry has had a difficult time responding to the competition from downloading. Vacuum cleaner manufacturers had to react when **Dyson** introduced its bagless cleaner (even though the Dyson was more expensive).

The result of competition can mean that a firm is simply no longer meeting consumer needs and customers switch to another firm. If this happens in large enough quantities then closure may be the end result.

Investigation

Identify one business that has failed – it might have closed down, been put into administration or is reported to be facing difficulties. Possible examples you might use that have had high-profile publicity are MG Rover, Golden Wonder Crisps and Farepak. Researching any of these via a search engine will give you plenty of information. You might also find examples of local businesses in your area that are struggling – a search of local press will be useful here.

1 Identify three reasons why you think that the business has failed.
2 Expand on each of the three reasons – use around 300 words for each one.
3 Which of the three reasons you have identified do you think is the most important factor in the failure of the business you have chosen? Explain your reasoning.

14 Why does the economy experience problems?

Introduction to economic activity

Every day, billions of people around the world go to work and engage in economic activity. This is all the buying and selling that goes on every day – billions and billions of decisions that are made by individuals. If you go into a shop and buy a packet of crisps, you are engaging in economic activity. You are one of the last people in the chain of production that has led to that packet of crisps being available. When you have finished eating the crisps there will still be some economic activity carried out afterwards, for example, the disposal of the waste packaging, which costs money to do.

The level of economic activity refers to the amount of buying and selling that goes on over a period of time. It is an important factor affecting the level of demand and supply. Buying and selling represents the process of production and exchange. It is not just about end users buying packets of crisps, but about all the buying and selling that goes on.

This includes the buying and selling that goes on between businesses. Hundreds of firms will be involved in the process of staging the Olympic Games in London in 2012. To take just one example, the construction of the main stadium will involve millions of transactions between firms all buying and selling different things. The stadium itself

The construction of a stadium involves many different businesses

will require huge quantities of steel and concrete. Someone has to produce the steel and concrete in the first place, and to extract the raw materials that are used to make them.

Slowdown in economic activity

A **slowdown** in economic activity means that there is less buying and selling going on. When a slowdown occurs, firms will cut back on production if their sales fall. When this happens, they may need fewer employees and so there may be redundancies. A general slowdown in economic activity usually causes a rise in unemployment.

If there is a slowdown in economic activity and unemployment is rising, those in work may also cut back their spending in case they face problems in the future. If you fear that you might be made unemployed you would think twice before borrowing to buy a new car or buying a new sofa on your credit card. The businesses that sell these products feel the effects of these decisions.

Economists recognise the importance of **expectations** in what happens to economic activity. If I think that the economy is going to slow down, I might cut back my spending. If there are lots of news stories in the papers and on TV about problems in the economy, it may feed through to our behaviour.

An increase in economic activity

The opposite can occur when the economy is growing. If there is more buying and selling going on, firms might hire more staff in order to meet the growing demand. When employment is rising, people have more income to spend and so demand rises further and the process continues.

We have mentioned that expectations can have a big effect on the level of economic activity. There are also two other major factors that we need to be aware of.

Interest rates

The interest rate is the price of borrowing money. Firms borrow money for buying new equipment and machinery and for expansion. Individuals borrow money to buy cars, washing machines, the latest widescreen plasma TV, holidays, house extensions, conservatories and much else.

Around 80 per cent of households in the UK have a mortgage – a loan granted specifically to buy a property. The repayment of the mortgage is usually a monthly one and can last for many years – 25 being a typical repayment period. It is the single biggest financial commitment that any individual is likely to take on. The mortgage payment is often a significant portion of monthly family expenditure.

If interest rates change, it will also change the cost of taking out a loan and a mortgage, and the cost of an existing loan or mortgage. This in turn has an effect on the amount of buying and selling. If interest rates fall, it encourages firms and individuals to take out more loans because they are cheaper and so results in more spending.

A rise in interest rates is likely to be accompanied by a slowdown in consumer spending. Most firms will see a fall in demand for their products or services as a result of this. Operating costs will also rise for every firm that has borrowings such as a loan or overdraft (the vast majority). Firms might decide to postpone decisions to invest in new equipment and machinery. When this happens, firms who might have been expecting orders for their products may see a fall in demand.

The international economy

What happens abroad can also have an important effect on some firms. If a firm relies for its revenue on selling goods or services to customers in other countries, then changes in world economic conditions may affect them badly. Possible factors include economic downturns abroad and disasters such as earthquakes, flood, drought and terrorist attack.

Investigation

1 Describe the trends in economic growth in the UK between 2001 and 2006.

2 Discuss some possible reasons for the trends that you have outlined.

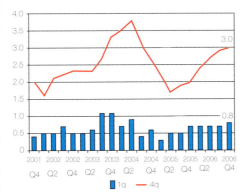

UK Economic Growth (GDP), 2001–2006 (%)

15 What does unemployment cost?

Introduction to unemployment

There are three different definitions of unemployment:

- 'those people currently out of work and actively seeking work'
- 'those persons out of work and actively seeking work and claiming benefit'
- 'those people out of work and available for employment'.

Each of these would give a different figure for the number of people unemployed. Not every unemployed person is able to claim benefit like Job Seekers Allowance (JSA), for example. Some people may be 'unemployed', but just between jobs.

So, if you are looking at unemployment in an investigation, you need to ensure that you are clear on which definition you are going to use.

The costs of unemployment

The costs of unemployment can be classified as those affecting an individual and those affecting society as a whole.

Costs to an individual

The costs to an individual may include:

- lack of a regular income – it is likely that income when unemployed is less than when employed
- loss of skills – the longer someone remains unemployed the less likely they are to maintain the skills necessary to secure employment
- loss of self-esteem – people may feel depressed when unemployed and feel that it is a personal rejection
- family problems – tensions over a lack of money and the self-esteem issue can lead to arguments within families and marital and family breakdowns
- possible involvement with crime – some unemployed people might be tempted to solve their financial problems by turning to crime.

Costs to society

Costs to society include:

- Higher state benefits – unemployed people need help and support so the state provides state payments such as JSA, housing benefits and so on. These represent a cost to the taxpayer. The higher the level of unemployment the higher the payments that need to be made and the more strain is put on tax revenue received by the government.
- Lower tax revenue – not only does unemployment lead to a rise in government expenditure but it is also likely to affect tax revenue. Unemployed people do not pay income tax and so this important source of government income is reduced.
- The opportunity cost – the opportunity cost to society of unemployment is the goods and services that could have been produced by those who are unemployed. Unemployed people represent productive resources and if they are not being used then society does not benefit from the products or services they could have produced if they had been working.
- The possible impact of crime – if unemployed people take up criminal activity, other people not immediately associated with the unemployment are affected.

Investigation

Read the following, then consider the task.

1 Unemployment can be hard to cope with, especially if you've been out of work for a long time.

2 Support services like Jobcentre Plus have a database of jobs that aims to find something that suits you.

3 If you're out of work, it's important to register a claim for benefit support as soon as possible, or you could be overwhelmed by accommodation and other living costs.

4 If you are looking for work, but unemployed or working less than 16 hours a week, you could claim JSA – but you are unlikely to get this if you're under 18 years old.

5 Schemes like the New Deal for Young People (aged 18–24) gives people claiming JSA access to a personal adviser, whose job is to help you get back to work.

Source: www.need2know.co.uk/work/unemployment

- Compare the costs to an individual of being unemployed to the costs to society. Give reasons for your arguments.

16 Can governments solve social and economic problems?

Introduction to government economic strategies

Governments spend a great deal of time putting in place policies and strategies to help reduce the effect of economic problems. Governments can provide training to help those who are unemployed find new work. They can help give people skills in interview technique, preparing CVs and completing application forms to help them find work. Equally important is providing information to unemployed people to help them find out what jobs are available, and putting companies in touch with those who are looking for work.

The government also provides advice and help to businesses who are looking to start up, expand, or move into international markets, through the Department of Trade and Industry. Politicians also try to change taxes and benefits to provide incentives to both consumers and producers to be enterprising and dynamic. In addition to this, the government itself is responsible for around 40 per cent of all spending in the economy, through its activities in the public sector. Changes in government spending can boost the level of economic activity or slow it down, depending on what the policy objective is.

There are several approaches a government can take in order to attempt to achieve its economic objectives:

Economic Objective	Possible Government Policy
To reduce the level of unemployment	■ Increase spending on job retraining schemes, to help people back into work ■ Increase Working Family Credits, to give a greater incentive to those who could find work, but don't bother
To increase the rate of growth in productivity	■ Special tax discounts for firms who invest in scientific research and technical development (R&D) ■ Encourage more people to start their own business enterprise, by offering more and better free advice to those thinking of starting up
To reduce regional inequalities	■ Spend on new motorways, e.g. motorways to Cornwall and to West Wales ■ Give special incentives to those starting up a new business in an area with a weak economy

Using government spending to solve social problems

There are several approaches a government can take in order to attempt to achieve its social objectives:

Social Objective	Possible Government Policy
Reduced inner-city crime	■ Increase spending on youth clubs and sports clubs ■ Increase spending on the police
Reduced obesity	■ Spend on a 'healthy living' advertising campaign ■ Increase research spending on the effects of eating fast foods
50 per cent of 18-year-olds achieving A Level standard	■ Increase spending on education (schools, teachers, etc.) ■ Offer students an income for staying at school after 16 (the EMA)

In 1997 the new Labour government made an important early decision. It handed control of **monetary policy** to the Bank of England. The Bank of England is the UK's central bank. It acts as banker to the government and oversees the whole of the banking system in the UK. In 1997 it was given responsibility for controlling inflation at a level which the government believes would help to keep the economy going in the right direction.

The Bank of England

At the time of writing (early 2007) the Bank of England has a target of 2 per cent for inflation. To influence the level of inflation, the Bank has responsibility for setting interest rates. If the Bank's key decision-makers think the level of economic activity is growing too fast, they might increase interest rates. If the economy is slowing down they might reduce interest rates to try to get the economy going again.

Investigation

Use the Office for National Statistics website (www.statistics.gov.uk) to find out what has happened to inflation over the last year.

1 Describe the trend in inflation over the last year.
2 Explain the factors that have caused inflation to have changed in the way you have identified.
3 Which of these factors do you think was the most significant reason for the change in inflation? Explain your reasoning.

Investigation

Find out what has happened to the interest rate in the UK over the last three years.

1 Explain what the reasons for the changes in the interest rate have been. (You can use the Bank of England's website for this, but you may find some of the language a bit tricky. You could also try searching on Biz/ed, at www.bized.co.uk.)
2 Can you observe a trend in the change in the interest rate (has it been generally rising, falling or staying the same)?
3 What do you think might have been the most important reason for the trends in the interest rate? Explain your reasoning.

SECTION 3

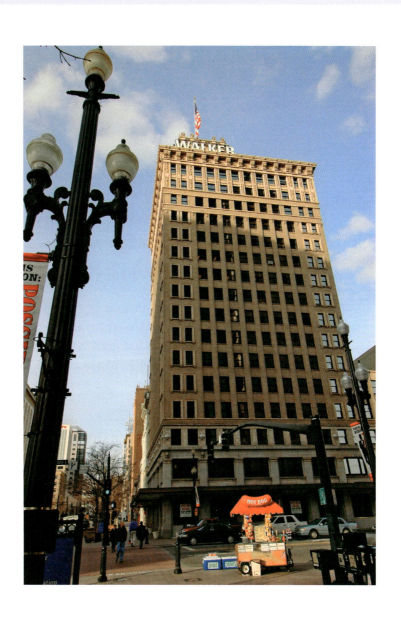

BIG OR SMALL?

17 How do firms grow?

There are two basic ways in which firms can grow. They can grow internally and externally. We will deal with both of these, in turn.

Internal growth

Internal growth refers to advances the firm achieves as a result of its own actions or decisions. Internal growth depends to a large extent on the firm making healthy profits and using those profits to help fund the growth of the firm. Using profits in this way involves an opportunity cost. By reinvesting the profits in the business, a sole trader is missing out on the opportunity to spend the money on other things. However, taking the profit now might mean sacrificing the long-term future of the business. It's a trade-off – immediate satisfaction against future stability for the business.

If the sole trader chose to put the profit back into the business, what would business growth actually look like? We need to distinguish between the short term and the long term. The short term is the period in which some factors of production cannot be changed, such as the maximum number of spectators at **Chelsea FC** (the ground cannot be enlarged overnight); in the long term, all factors of production can be altered. An example is the best way to illustrate this.

Small business growth

Jilly is an experienced hair stylist. She made a decision to set up her own hairdressing business in 1997. She bought a small shop in a small town in the south-west of England and began trading. In this shop she had limited space and facilities. She employed another stylist, Sue, and together the two built up their client base. After a year it became obvious that the shop was too small. Jilly had to turn potential customers away because the shop lacked the resources to be able to see them.

Jilly only had two basins where hair could be washed, two chairs for styling hair, a cramped waiting area, limited facilities for making coffee and tea and a small toilet for customers. In addition there were only the two staff. Jilly made the decision to increase the number of staff at the salon. She employed a junior whose job it would be to wash clients' hair, sweep up, keep the salon clean, make coffee and tea and sort out the laundry. Jilly's business had started to grow.

In the short run, Jilly knew that she could employ more people to help out at the salon. She could look at reorganising the salon, but ultimately she knew that if the business was to grow further that she would have to increase all the factors of production. That would mean not only employing more staff but having more wash basins and more places to deal with customers. Ultimately, this meant getting a bigger shop. When a business expands by moving to new premises or opening new outlets, they are experiencing long-run growth.

How long is the short run and how long is the long run? That is a difficult question to answer. It all depends on how long it will take to change all the factors of production. If the government decided that it needed to increase the capacity of the electricity supply industry then it might be that the long run would be ten years – the amount of time it might take to build a new power station. For Jilly, the long run was the amount of time it took to find new premises and buy all the equipment needed for the new premises as well as hiring new stylists.

New premises do not just appear when you want them. Even if somewhere does turn up it may not be suitable – it might not be in the right place to attract customers; it might have too much work needing to be done to it to make it right for a hairdressing salon; it might be too close to a competitor and so on. It took Jilly around 18 months to find suitable new premises – big enough to cope with the customers that Jilly thought she could get, but affordable.

The new premises allowed Jilly to have a separate area where clients could wait, an area where they could get their hair washed, space for a reception area and for five styling positions. She had to hire extra staff and eventually had five full-time and three part-time staff.

From opening a small shop employing just two people, Jilly had expanded to a larger salon with eight people employed. The business had grown. How well the business does in the future will depend very much on how the initial expansion goes. It is not a case of opening the bigger salon and then next year another one and then another. It might take five years to build the reputation that can be used to justify opening another salon in a different town. The long run in this instance would be five years – the time it would take to expand all of the factors of production again.

It is possible that Jilly's business could grow into a national chain of hairdressing salons – every town and city might end up having a 'Jilly's' somewhere in it. Yet sustained growth tends to happen to only a very small number of the businesses that start up in the UK every year. Getting to the stage of a Tesco or a WH Smith is not easy and takes many years.

Innovation and new product development

Some businesses achieve internal growth because they develop new products and services that become very popular and increase sales. New products may be improvements on existing products. For example, mobile phones have come a long way since the large bulky and often inefficient mobile phones that first appeared in the 1980s.

To try and boost sales, firms try to find ways of persuading customers to buy new phones. If a company develops the capability of having a mobile phone that allows people to watch high quality TV pictures, maybe this will help the business to grow. Once you have a winning formula, however, the work does not stop there. It is essential that businesses keep looking for the next 'big idea' if they are to maintain sales and continue to grow in the future.

How do we measure business growth?

We have seen in the example of Jilly's salon how a business might grow in both the short and long run. Many firms will grow in exactly this way – some might grow quicker than others but the principle is the same. Measuring business growth can be done in a variety of different ways – you might look at some or all of these factors in assessing the extent to which a firm is growing.

Revenue

A firm's growth might be measured through how its revenue is increasing. **Revenue** is the amount the firm receives from selling its output. If revenue is increasing from one year to the next we can say that the firm is growing.

Sales volume

This is closely related to revenue. Sales volume measures the actual amount of goods or services sold. For a firm like **Cadbury Schweppes**, sales volume might be measuring the number of bars of Cadbury's Whole Nut sold in a year. For Jilly, it might be the number of clients dealt with over a period of a year. If these volumes are growing each year, again, we can say that the firm is growing.

Profit

Profit can be used as a measure of business growth. We do have to be careful, however, when looking at profit. If we compare two businesses, one making a profit of £500,000 and another making a profit of £250,000, can we say that the firm making the bigger profit is bigger or is experiencing growth? Possibly, but not necessarily. We would have to look at other factors as well. The reason is **profit margin** – the difference between the cost of production and the price of the good or service. Some firms sell large volumes with small margins, while others sell low volumes with large margins. The two might make exactly the same profit, however! We can make more of a judgement about the growth of an individual firm if we compare its profit from year to year. If profit levels are growing then we might conclude that the firm is growing.

Capital assets

Capital is the equipment and machinery that a business uses to aid production. Large businesses often have very large capital assets. Take a business like **Asda**. There are over 300 Asda food stores in the UK. In each food store there is a massive array of shelves, tills, equipment, machinery, not to mention the fleets of lorries and distribution centres dotted around the country. All these capital assets are a far cry from the small beginnings of the business in the early 1920s. Therefore the value of a firm's capital assets are a measure of its size, and comparing its capital assets over a period give some clues as to the growth of a business.

How is internal growth financed?

Internal growth tends to be financed by the business ploughing back profits made into the business to help it grow. This can be a slow process and does, of course, depend on the level of profits being made by the business. Putting back profits into the business means new equipment can be purchased, more labour can be employed and expansion can be paid for.

The purchase of new equipment and labour can mean that the firm can become more efficient. What we mean by this is that the firm can produce the same amount at lower cost or can produce more for the same cost. Either way the business hopes to be able to increase sales, improve its profits and use that to expand even more.

Retained profit is the term used to describe the profits set aside for re-investment into the business. Firms can also use other sources of finance to fund expansion. Bank loans are often used to purchase equipment and machinery. Obtaining a loan from a bank does mean that the business will have to pay back not only the amount borrowed (the capital sum) but also interest. The rate of interest for small businesses can be quite high and if interest rates rise then the firm faces increased costs. Retained profit is not necessarily better. In most cases, the ideal is a combination of finance: using both reinvested profit and some bank loans.

External growth

Many firms have grown through a combination of internal and external growth. External growth occurs when a firm grows by buying up other businesses. These businesses may, or may not, be similar to the original business.

External growth occurs mostly through a merger or takeover. A merger occurs when two firms agree to join together. The resulting firm retains some form of identity of both original businesses. Cadbury, for example, merged with drinks company Schweppes to form Cadbury Schweppes.

A **takeover** occurs where one business gains control over another. The takeover may not be welcomed by the firm being bought. A takeover succeeds when one firm gains a 51 per cent stake in another. **Morrisons**, for example, bought the Safeway supermarket chain. Within two years all the Safeway stores had been renamed Morrisons, or sold off.

Mergers and takeovers are important methods of business growth. In order to see why firms might choose this sort of growth rather than internal growth we need to identify different types of merger or takeover.

Business sectors

Businesses can be classified according to the sector of production that they operate in. These sectors are primary, secondary or tertiary:

- The **primary sector** is associated with mining, quarrying, agriculture and fishing and any business that is involved in the extraction of raw materials from the earth.
- **Secondary production** refers to processing and manufacturing – turning raw materials into other products that may be sold either to consumers or to other businesses.
- The **tertiary sector** is also known as the service sector. This includes businesses involved in finance, banking, insurance, retail, entertainment, distribution and so on.

A business might have grown within one particular sector but can see benefits of buying a business in another sector. For example, **BP** is a business associated with oil. Processing oil into different products like petrol, diesel and jet fuel is part of the secondary stage. BP might have relied on oil producers operating in the primary sector for supplies of oil. It makes sense for them to try and buy oil fields and take control of the actual extraction of oil. Equally, it might be of benefit to BP to be able to have control over the sale of the petrol it produces. Buying petrol station forecourts, therefore, may be a sensible way of the business growing.

A takeover of a business at a different stage of the same productive process is called a **vertical takeover**. BP might buy an oil-drilling business in Nigeria. The secondary producer (BP) would be buying a primary producer (the oil-drilling business). If it took over a chain of petrol stations owned by a private business, it would be buying a business in the tertiary sector. BP wants to control every link in the chain, from oil discovery and drilling, through to petrol sales at a garage near you. Other companies, such as **Mars**, are happy to operate in just one sector. Mars manufactures chocolates (and pet food), but does not choose to buy up its suppliers (in the primary sector) or its retail customers (in the tertiary sector).

Some businesses look to buy other businesses at the same stage of the production process. Asda was bought by the giant American retailer **Wal-Mart** in 1999. Wal-Mart made a bid of £6.7 billion to buy Asda. This is known as a **horizontal takeover**. In this case, both Wal-Mart and Asda are in the tertiary sector. A horizontal merger or takeover means buying up one of your competitors.

Reasons for external growth:

- increasing sales
- increasing revenue
- moving into new markets
- gaining expertise
- obtaining a well known and respected brand
- increasing market share
- reducing risk (diversification)
- securing a source of supply
- securing a market outlet.

The above could all be possible reasons for buying another business. It is unlikely that there will only be one reason; it will generally be a combination of several factors.

Investigation

Try to find a local small business that would be prepared to talk to you. Arrange an interview with the owner and find out the following information:

- When did the business start?
- How did the business start?
- What finance did the owner need to get started?
- Has the business grown and if so, in what way?
- What plans does the owner have for future business growth? How long is this likely to take (if relevant)?

From your investigation, write a summary report on the most important factor (so far) that led to the growth of the business you have investigated.

Investigation

A lot of merger and takeover activity goes on in the financial world. Choose an example of a merger or takeover that has either happened in the past year or is in the process of happening.

1 Investigate the reasons why the takeover took place. Give at least three reasons.

2 Which of the reasons you have given do you think was the most important or significant one? Explain why you chose that one.

18 Monopoly power – good or bad?

Market share and market power

In any market there are a number of businesses. In some markets there are hundreds of businesses, each of which might be a small sole trader or private limited company. In other markets, there might be many firms but the market might be dominated by a relatively small number of very large public limited companies.

An example of an industry that has many small sole traders is plumbing. Each area of the country is likely to have dozens of self-employed plumbers. The total number of plumbing firms in the UK, therefore, runs into the thousands. In the grocery market (selling food, fruit, vegetables and so on) there are also hundreds of small firms. The market, however, is dominated by a small number of very big firms – the giant supermarkets that we all know.

If we take the total sales in the market as a whole and then look at the percentage of those sales that an individual firm accounts for, we can get some idea of the structure of the market – how it is made up.

Market share

The percentage of total sales accounted for by a firm is referred to as the **market share**.

In the grocery market, the big four, **Asda**, **Tesco**, **Sainsbury** and **Morrisons**, account for almost 75 per cent of the total sales of food

and groceries in the UK. The small corner shop or village greengrocer is still part of the market but is tiny in comparison.

Many businesses are keen to increase their market share. An increased market share is associated with a greater degree of **market power**. Market power occurs when a firm is able to have some control over the market. A powerful firm might be able to control supply, influence prices, affect choice or somehow affect the way that other businesses operate.

Many local greengrocers have complained that the opening of a large supermarket has caused their sales to fall and forced them to close down. Farmers complain that their major buyers are the supermarkets and that they are so big that the farmer is at the mercy of these big powerful businesses. If the farmer does not like the prices that a supermarket is offering them for their crops, are they in a position to complain? Many farmers feel that if they complain the supermarket will simply go elsewhere. It is as if the farmer needs the supermarket more than the supermarket needs the individual farmer.

Are some firms too big?

The size of some businesses has led to complaints that some firms have too much market power. Too much market power implies that competition is not working as it should. In a competitive market, there are lots of firms all trying to persuade customers to buy their product or service rather than that of their rivals. **Competition** tends to lead to firms charging lower prices, offering better quality goods and services and being more efficient than if there is limited competition.

This is pretty much common sense. If you are the only person selling a particular product, you could get away with charging higher prices than if there are many all selling a similar product. If you are the only seller, what is to stop you from offering lower-quality products for sale? Also, what incentive is there for you to keep costs down?

When firms have market power, they are sometimes referred to as **monopolies**. The word 'monopoly' means one seller. In theory, therefore, a monopoly is a single seller of a good or service in a market. After the Second World War, a number of important industries were **nationalised** (moved into the control of the state). Electricity, gas, coal, steel and telephones were all state monopolies. You either bought your telephone from the GPO (who ran the telephone system at that time) or went without.

In most markets, however, even if there is only one seller, it does not mean that there is no competition whatsoever. If gas were still provided by one firm, you might think they had a monopoly in energy supplies. In one respect they would. But electricity is also a source of energy, and so is coal. There is generally some element of choice in every market. However, it may be difficult for consumers to be able to switch to an alternative. Electric central heating may be in competition to gas central heating but it is very difficult, and costly, for a customer to just switch from electric central heating to gas central heating.

Because of the concerns over market power, the government has a target maximum level of market share. Any firm with a market share of over 25 per cent may be subject to investigation about the way it conducts its business. This 25 per cent figure, therefore, is a measure of monopoly power. If two firms wish to join together, or if there is a takeover planned, the government will be watching what happens to the market share of the two companies.

In 2004, **Morrisons** was successful in a bid to take over Safeway. Tesco and Asda had also put in bids, but as the two biggest supermarkets it was very unlikely that either of these would have been allowed to take over Safeway. Morrisons was a smaller business and the combined market share of Morrisons and Safeway was not considered to be damaging to competition in the industry.

We need to be very careful, therefore, when we are talking about monopoly power. In general, if there are concerns that a firm is behaving in a way that limits competition and does not act in the public interest, then it may be investigated for abusing its monopoly power.

Monopoly power: a bad thing?

The concerns about public interest and abuse of monopoly power are associated with the disadvantages of firms having monopoly power. These disadvantages are:

- The effect on prices: firms with monopoly power are likely to charge higher prices than would be the case if there was greater competition.
- The effect on choice: the fewer firms there are in a market the less choice the customer has. If customers are not happy with one firm's prices or service, they want to switch to a competitor. If a firm is able to exercise monopoly power then this choice is restricted. Firms with monopoly power know that and might not offer the best value for money for the customer.
- The effect on new firms entering the industry: when firms are very big and have monopoly power, they might be able to make it difficult for new firms to enter the industry. These 'barriers to entry' include the use of patents and copyright – as is used by **Apple** to protect its highly profitable iTunes service.

Monopoly power: a good thing?

Firms who are able to exercise monopoly power are often assumed to be negative in their effects. The disadvantages of firms having monopoly power can certainly bring problems that may not be in the public interest. There are, however, advantages that can arise of firms who have some form of monopoly power.

When carrying out any sort of investigation into monopoly power, you must be sure to provide some balance to your argument and look for some of the benefits that might arise. These benefits are summarised below.

Value for money for customers

Firms with high market share are able to negotiate good prices with suppliers and can pass these lower prices onto consumers. Food in supermarkets in the UK is currently cheaper in real terms than it was 20 years ago. The buying power of the likes of Tesco and Asda are a significant reason for this.

Innovation and new product development

Developing new products and getting them to the market can take many years and millions of pounds in investment. Without some form of guarantee of monopoly power, many firms would not have the incentive to invest in such development. This is particularly relevant to the pharmaceutical industries (who produce medicines and drugs). Developing new drugs costs huge sums of money and may take anything up to 20 years, and even longer in some cases. Such firms do require some form of incentive to undertake this long-term and very risky investment. Their incentive is that their new drugs can be patented, to prevent others from copying their invention.

Efficiency

Some large firms can be more efficient than smaller ones. They may be able to afford to buy specialist machinery that increases the amount produced but lowers their unit costs. For example, if we that assume a product currently costs £100,000 to produce and a firm is currently producing 100,000 of these items, the unit cost is £1 per item. If a machine is available that increases output by 300 per cent (to 300,000) but which increased total cost by only 100 per cent (to £200,000) then the unit costs will be 200,000/300,000 = 66p. Firms who are able to reduce their unit costs in this way can gain a competitive advantage over their rivals and possibly reduce prices for consumers.

Natural monopolies

Some types of production need large firms to be able to do it efficiently. In addition, some types of production would generate massive waste if there were too many firms all trying to provide a similar product. Such products or services might rely on nationwide networks of capital equipment – such as telephone lines, electricity pylons, water pipes and so on. It would be very wasteful of resources if there were 20 electricity firms all trying to build electricity supply networks across the country!

Investigation

Choose a business that you think has some form of monopoly power.

1 Explain why you think the firm has monopoly power and how it exhibits signs of having monopoly power.

2 Identify and explain the advantages and disadvantages of the monopoly power of your chosen business.

3 Do you think that the advantages of the firm having monopoly power outweigh the disadvantages? Explain your reasons.

19 Can we control the giants?

The growth of the supermarkets has provided most members of the population of the UK with an unprecedented choice of goods and services at reasonable prices and of high quality. That is the benefit. The cost has been the effect on other stakeholders – suppliers, the local community and small businesses that cannot compete.

When looking at monopolies we have to consider the trade-off – do the advantages that firms with monopoly power like the supermarkets have outweigh the disadvantages? When is an appropriate time to decide that these firms have got too big? That is the job of the regulator.

Regulation

Regulators are independent bodies set up by the government to oversee the behaviour and activities of businesses and organisations. The major regulatory bodies that are relevant to this section of your course are the **Competition Commission** and the regulators of the former nationalised industries like gas, electricity, water, the railways and the telephones.

> **The Office of Gas and Electricity Markets (Ofgem)**
>
> This body oversees businesses supplying gas and electricity to consumers. It has powers to fine firms who it believes are acting against the public interest, e.g. price-fixing. Ofgem can investigate the prices that these firms set and look at the impact of the industry on the environment. Ofgem is supposed to act in the interests of customers, including those who are disabled or on low incomes.

Ofgem is a typical example of one of the regulators that monitor the activities of an industry that used to be a state monopoly. Because of the nature of these industries, the extent of the competition that has been created is limited. That is why the government set up these regulators when these industries were privatised in the 1980s and

1990s. **Privatisation** means the transfer of state-owned businesses to the private sector.

Privatised industries tend to be those where the public relies on the products and services for everyday living, such as water or gas. If firms in these industries were allowed to use their full monopoly power, ordinary households might face huge problems. Imagine what would happen if your local water company increased its prices by 1,000 per cent. Would you have any choice to go and use a different water supply company? The answer is basically 'No'. That is why bodies like Ofgem and **Ofwat** (The Office of the Water Regulator) have been set up.

In reality, few firms are likely to raise their prices so excessively that they price consumers out of the market. What the regulator will be looking at will be the extent of any price rises by such firms. Is a 2 per cent price increase for our annual water bills too much or are they justified by the need to invest in improving water quality and supplies? How about 5 per cent; or 10 per cent? What is a justified price rise for firms who have such monopoly power? The job of the regulator is to investigate the arguments on both sides and to arrive at judgements about how the industry should be operating.

Many firms who might have some form of monopoly power are not former nationalised industries. If there are concerns that these firms might be exploiting their monopoly powers, the Competition Commission can be called in to investigate.

The Competition Commission came into existence with the passing of the **Competition Act** in 1998. It investigates mergers, markets and industries when a concern has been passed to it. This might arise as a result of a complaint by a member of the public or another business through other bodies like the **Office of Fair Trading**. As a result of its investigations, the Commission will provide recommendations with regard to the case. These recommendations have to be acted upon by the firm/s concerned.

For example, in November 2006, the Commission published its findings into an investigation into the proposed takeover between Hamsard 2786 Limited and Academy Music Holdings Limited. These two companies own various live music venues in London. Hamsard own the Mean Fiddler, The Astoria and The Forum and also have interests in the Wembley Arena and links to the Hammersmith Apollo. Academy owns the Shepherds Bush Empire, the Brixton Academy and other smaller venues in London.

The Commission decided that the takeover would restrict competition and possibly lead to higher prices for artists who wanted to hire these venues to perform in. They also felt that the quality of the service provided by these venues would fall.

As a result of its findings, the Commission recommended two alternative 'remedies' (ways of solving the problem) so that competition would not be affected:

1 Prevent the takeover from happening.
2 Allow the takeover to go ahead but make the resulting business sell off some of the venues in London to avoid too great a concentration of monopoly power.

The European Union and regulation

Businesses are not only affected by regulators in the UK, the EU also has bodies that oversee competition in markets across Europe. The EU Competition Commission does much the same work as the UK Competition Commission but its work is related to competition issues that affect Europe as a whole rather than an individual country.

One high-profile case that has been going on for some years now is between **Microsoft** and the EU Competition Commission. The EU has accused Microsoft of anti-competitive behaviour. It believes that Microsoft is using its market power to restrict competition. Microsoft's operating system, Windows, is used on over 80 per cent of computers around the world. Microsoft also provides other software within its operating system such as Media Player and Internet Explorer (its web browser).

By bundling all these different products together, Microsoft is accused of preventing other firms who could provide media players or browsers from competing. The EU competition authorities have ordered Microsoft to allow rivals to develop software to run on Windows. Microsoft doesn't believe that it is restricting competition and does not want to help its competitors. The EU imposed a fine on Microsoft of £1.4 million per day if Microsoft failed to comply with its ruling.

Self-regulation?

The existence of bodies such as Ofwat and the Competition Commission are meant to discourage firms from taking advantage of their monopoly powers. By having these organisations, it is hoped that firms will regulate their own behaviour and act in responsible ways.

Firms are also mindful that a powerful position today might fall away tomorrow. Businesses rise and fall like empires! If they do not keep looking over their shoulder, then there is the chance that they could start to face competition from other firms.

This and the existence of the authorities like the Competition Commission will, it is hoped, provide sufficient incentive for firms to think twice before they try to exploit any monopoly power they might have. There are those who would argue, however, some multinational businesses are too big to be worried by the threat of regulatory bodies.

The decision about how to control the giants comes down to a trade-off. Large firms bring benefits to society and the economy but there might come a time when they become so big that they are able to wield too much power. Where that point lies is a matter of judgement!

Investigation

Go to the website of the Competition Commission, or one of the privatised industry regulators such as Ofwat, Ofrail or Ofgem. These sorts of sites usually have a section that tells the public about investigations into complaints that they have been involved with. Choose one such example.

1 Briefly summarise the arguments linked to the case you have chosen.
2 Evaluate the outcome of the case.

Investigation

Go to the EU competition website at:
http://ec.europa.eu/comm/competition/index_en.html

There are a series of sections in this site about mergers and anti-competitive practices.

1 Choose one of the sections and look at the 'news' section. Select one of the cases that the EU has been involved in – one about a business that you are interested in or aware of.
2 Why was the EU Competition Commission involved in the case?
3 Discuss the issues that arise from the case that you have chosen in relation to monopoly power.

Investigation

1 Choose one firm that is a dominant business in its market. (Tesco and Microsoft are possible examples but you are free to choose your own.)
2 Write a report or create a presentation based around the following question: To what extent has the firm you have chosen become too big in the market it is operating?

SECTION 4

CREATE OR DESTROY?

20 How do we measure standard of living?

It does not take an economist to appreciate the difference in these two photographs. One shows people who have clearly got 'lots of money' and the other, people who have very little. Money allows us to be able to buy the things in life that we need – food, water, clothing and shelter – and also lots of things that we want but that are not essential to our survival.

The owners of the yacht are clearly hugely rich. What more could they possibly want to buy for themselves? For the people in the second image, there are probably many, quite simple things, which would make life much better. We compare these material possessions when we talk about **standard of living**.

Standard of living can refer to the amount of goods and services people in a country have access to – what they are able to buy. It can also refer to the way that people live. The first definition means that we have to look at information about money and material possessions as the basis for our measure. The second might mean looking at different information that helps us to build a picture of what life might be like for people living in a country.

What people can buy is closely linked to the level of **income** that they receive – what they earn or money they get from other sources (for example, money they have inherited or from investments they have made). Income levels are an important factor in determining a person's standard of living.

We can compare the standard of living in different countries. We can make statements like 'the standard of living in the UK is higher than that in Malawi'.

Measuring the standard of living

We can measure the standard of living in several different ways. For example, we can look at some of the luxuries that are available to individuals in a country. How many TVs are there in your home? Do you have a TV in your bedroom? You are likely to have a bed, more than one set of clothes and other personal possessions (such as jewellery or a bicycle). Maybe you also have one or more of the following: a Playstation, an MP3 player, a PC or laptop.

Looking at the number of people in a country that has access to these types of things is one way to measure the standard of living. If you have any of the things in the lists above then your standard of living is far higher than almost everyone your age living in a country like Sierra Leone in Africa.

You might see references to the number of TVs per 100 people in the country or the number of cars per household as ways of comparing living standards between countries. You could argue that a TV might be considered vital to our way of life in the UK today. In reality, there are many more important things that determine living standards.

Access to clean water, access to medical care and access to education are all be considered to be important in providing a decent quality of life. They are often things that we, in the UK, might take for granted. In some countries, access to health care, education and clean water are poor, or do not exist at all.

Different perspectives about the standard of living

We have to be careful to remember the importance of perspectives in discussing topics like the standard of living. I might consider an MP3 player an essential part of my life – a must-have gadget. When we include different items as a means of comparing countries – the number of TVs, fridges, washing machines and so on – we are using our opinion about what constitutes a decent standard of living.

Some people do not agree that having a car or the latest plasma screen TV is that important in life. They see the standard of living defined in a different way. Economists are increasingly becoming interested in the economics of happiness. Countries that have very high standards of living, as defined by the number of material goods they have, also have lots of problems associated with them – crime, stress, pressured living and so on. We might have lots of material possessions, but does that make us happy?

When comparing standards of living, we need to be careful that we bear in mind that any definition of the standard of living carries with it a judgement about what constitutes a decent life. Simon Fairlie might be one good example of someone who would not see traditional definitions of standards of living as being necessarily accurate. Simon and a group of similar- minded people live on a 40-acre site called Tinker's Bubble which comprises woodland, orchards and pasture land. The eight adults and four children are almost entirely self-sufficient. They have an alternative lifestyle. They produce much of their own food, and are able to generate electricity from solar and wind power.

Communal living in this way may not be everyone's choice, but the residents at Tinker's Bubble help us to understand that the traditional view of a 'good' standard of living is not the only view, or necessarily the right one.

The Human Development Index

Because measuring the standard of living can be difficult, different ways of being able to compare living standards in countries have been developed. One such measure is called the Human Development Index (HDI). The HDI is produced by a branch of the United Nations called the United Nations Development Programme. It looks at standards of living based on the following measures in different countries:

- life expectancy (the average number of years an individual can expect to live)
- literacy rates (the number of people who can read and write)
- the average number of years of education that an individual receives
- gross domestic product (GDP) – the value of the output produced in one year by a country.

Below is an extract from the 2006 HDI Report published by the UNDP in November 2006.

HDI rank [a]		Human development index (HDI) value 2004	Life expectancy at birth (years) 2004	Adult literacy rate [b] (% ages 15 and older) 2004	Combined gross enrolment ratio for primary, secondary and tertiary schools (%) 2004 [c]	GDP per capita (PPP US$) 2004
HIGH HUMAN DEVELOPMENT						
1	Norway	0.965	79.6	.. [e]	100 [f]	38,454
2	Iceland	0.960	80.9	.. [e]	96 [g]	33,051
3	Australia	0.957	80.5	.. [e]	113 [f]	30,331
4	Ireland	0.956	77.9	.. [e]	99	38,827
5	Sweden	0.951	80.3	.. [e]	96	29,541
6	Canada	0.950	80.2	.. [e]	93 [g, h]	31,263
7	Japan	0.949	82.2	.. [e]	85	29,251
8	United States	0.948	77.5	.. [e]	93	39,676
9	Switzerland	0.947	80.7	.. [e]	86	33,040
10	Netherlands	0.947	78.5	.. [e]	98	31,789
11	Finland	0.947	78.7	.. [e]	100 [f]	29,951
12	Luxembourg	0.945	78.6	.. [e]	85 [h, i]	69,961 [j]
13	Belgium	0.945	79.1	.. [e]	95	31,096
14	Austria	0.944	79.2	.. [e]	91	32,276
15	Denmark	0.943	77.3	.. [e]	101 [f]	31,914
16	France	0.942	79.6	.. [e]	93	29,300
17	Italy	0.940	80.2	98.4 [e]	89	28,180
18	United Kingdom	0.940	78.5	.. [e]	93 [g]	30,821
19	Spain	0.938	79.7	98.0 [e, k]	96	25,047
20	New Zealand	0.936	79.3	.. [e]	100 [f]	23,413
160	Guinea	0.445	53.9	29.5	42	2,180
161	Angola	0.439	41.0	67.4	26 [g, h]	2,180 [p]
162	Tanzania, U. Rep. of	0.430	45.9	69.4	48 [g]	674
163	Benin	0.428	54.3	34.7	49 [g]	1,091
164	Côte d'Ivoire	0.421	45.9	48.7	40 [g, h]	1,551
165	Zambia	0.407	37.7	68.0 [o]	54 [g]	943
166	Malawi	0.400	39.8	64.1 [o]	64 [g]	646
167	Congo, Dem. Rep. of the	0.391	43.5	67.2	27 [g, h]	705 [p]
168	Mozambique	0.390	41.6	.. [l]	49	1,237 [p]
169	Burundi	0.384	44.0	59.3	36	677 [p]
170	Ethiopia	0.371	47.8	.. [l]	36	756 [p]
171	Chad	0.368	43.7	25.7	35 [g]	2,090 [p]
172	Central African Republic	0.353	39.1	48.6	30 [g, h]	1,094 [p]
173	Guinea-Bissau	0.349	44.8	.. [l]	37 [g, h]	722 [p]
174	Burkina Faso	0.342	47.9	21.8	26 [g]	1,169 [p]
175	Mali	0.338	48.1	19.0 [o]	35	998
176	Sierra Leone	0.335	41.0	35.1	65 [g]	561 [p]
177	Niger	0.311	44.6	28.7	21	779 [p]

(Source: United Nations Development Programme, Human Development Report 2006, Palgrave Macmillan, reproduced with permission of Palgrave Macillan)

This shows the top 20 countries and the bottom 18. The differences between the standards of living of the very top and the very bottom of the index are stark. The bottom 18 are all African states. The difference in the average life expectancy is startling. The average person in Niger will live for just 44.6 years. Compare this to Norway, where the average person can look forward to 79.6 years of life. Only 28.7 per cent of Niger's population can read and write and only 21 per cent attend primary, secondary and tertiary education. The average income, as shown by the GDP figure per head of the population, shows that the average income per head in Norway is over $38,000 a year; in Niger it is just $779 a year.

We can combine statistics like the HDI with other data to measure the standard of living, such as:

- the number of fridges per head of the population
- the number of TVs per head of the population
- information about how common certain diseases are
- crime levels
- stress levels.

We can build up a good picture of the standard of living of people in those countries.

Why is measuring the standard of living important?

Compared to the 1800s, the vast majority of people in the UK can look forward to a considerably more comfortable life than was the case then. People have access to health care, education, material possessions, and a basic mobility infrastructure (like roads, railways and so on) that all help to contribute to the quality of life. Not to mention, of course, the availability of essentials like food, clothing, water and housing.

It can be argued that all these things lead to a better quality of life and that it is desirable to see improvements in the standard of living of the population – however this is measured. It also helps those in power who make decisions on our behalf to try to rectify areas of concern and to create the right conditions for improvements in living standards.

Measuring the standard of living also helps us to be able to appreciate those countries where living standards are quite different. The United Nations have established what are called Millennium Development Goals (MDGs) to try to focus the attention of the world on the needs of the poorest nations on earth. These goals are:

1 Eradicate extreme poverty and hunger.
2 Achieve universal primary education.
3 Promote gender equality and empower women.
4 Reduce child mortality.
5 Improve maternal health.
6 Combat HIV/AIDS, malaria and other diseases.
7 Ensure environmental sustainability.
 (Source: www.un.org/millenniumgoals/index.html)

The Millenium Goals are very challenging, especially given the time frame that the UN has set – 2015. However, if they can be met, it is widely agreed that the lives of millions of people around the world will have been improved. In short, they will have a better standard of living.

Useful websites

UN Millennium Development Goals
www.un.org/millenniumgoals/index.html
The United Nations Development Programme HDI Report, 2006
http://hdr.undp.org/hdr2006/

The CIA World Factbook
https://www.cia.gov/cia/publications/factbook/index.html
The Organisation for Economic Cooperation and Development (OECD)
www.oecd.org

Investigation

1 Do some research to find the top ten richest nations in the world and the bottom ten, as measured by GDP per capita.
2 To what extent is this measure a satisfactory way of measuring the standard of living of the people in the countries you have identified?

Investigation

Using measures that look at what we are able to buy is just one way of looking at living standards. The Tinker's Bubble experiment looks at living standards from a different perspective. Research the Tinker's Bubble experiment on the Internet, then write a report that evaluates the two ways of looking at living standards.

21 Economic growth

What is economic growth?

An economy is made up of all the buying and selling that goes on between businesses, individuals and governments. We can measure this economic activity in three ways:

- the amount people spend – their expenditure
- the amount people earn – their income
- the value of the goods and services produced – the output.

In theory, each of these should add up to the same amount. If I agree to buy two tickets for a Robbie Williams concert from you for £100, my expenditure has been £100. Your income is the amount you have earned from selling the tickets, which is also £100. The value of the output is the price of the two tickets, which is…£100!

This is a very simple example of just one buying and selling activity. If we were able to add up all the buying and selling that went on in a country over a period of time we would, in theory, be able to get a measure of the level of economic activity over that period.

If we compared this figure with that calculated in the previous year, we would get a measure of the economic growth in a country over that time. For example, the total amount spent on goods and services in the UK in 2004 was £1,187,000 million (that's 1.1 trillion). By 2005 the figure had risen to £1,215,000 million. This shows that the economy experienced some economic growth.

We know that £1,215,000 million is a bigger sum than £1,187,000 million but clearly, sums of money like these are impossible to fully understand and appreciate. It is easier, therefore, to look at the **percentage changes** in economic activity over a period. This shows us the growth rate of economic activity.

In the example above, the growth rate was 2.35 per cent. This means that there was an increase in the amount of spending, or income or output of around 2.35 per cent compared to the previous year. In the UK, a growth rate of between 2 per cent and 3 per cent a year would be considered about right for the size of our economy. However, in

China growth rates of 9–10 per cent per year have been typical of the last few years.

Looking at rates of growth is important in understanding what is happening to an economy. It is also important to get to grips with some basic arithmetic. If economic growth in the UK was 2.6 per cent in 2004 and 2.3 per cent in 2005, would that mean the level of economic activity had fallen? The answer is 'no'. The rate at which the economy was growing had slowed down but economic growth was still positive. The level of economy activity rose by 2.6 per cent in 2004 and a further 2.3 per cent in 2005. In 2005, however, the rate of growth was not as fast as it was in 2004.

It is possible for economic growth to really fall. This would be expressed as a negative number. For example, if GDP in 2005 was £1,215,000 million and in 2006 was reported as being £1,200,000 million, we would say that the economy had 'shrunk'. We would be producing fewer goods and services in 2006 that we did in 2005. In this example, the rate of economic growth would be -1.23 per cent. So it is important to look carefully at GDP figures and check what the data are telling you.

How does economic growth occur?

To get some understanding of this we need to look at our definition of GDP. We defined it as the value of output produced by an economy in a given time period – usually one year. We need to count up all the goods and services produced during one year in the UK and multiply the figure by the price that these goods and services were sold at. This would show that year's GDP – the value of the country's output.

We said that economic activity can be measured either by looking at total spending (expenditure), total income or the value of output. In theory they should all be the same. If economic growth is to occur we need to see an increase in spending and therefore incomes. How does this happen?

There are a number of factors that can lead to economic growth. Imagine a plot of land which has just two people – a male and a female – living on it. The couple have to try to feed themselves from the land. Let us assume we start at a time period we will call Year 1. In Year 1 the couple manage to sow some corn seed but various problems mean that they don't produce much food for themselves. They know that they will have to keep some of the seed back in order to get a harvest next year, but in the process they go hungry for much of the year.

In the next year things improve slightly. The harvest is better as a result of the right weather and the couple find that they have enough to feed themselves, to buy a spade and a hoe, and be able to have enough seed to sow for next year. This improves their productivity and they are able to produce a very healthy crop in the next year. They put aside enough to feed themselves and also an amount to sow for next year, leaving a small surplus. They use this to trade with a nearby couple for some seed potatoes. Pleased that they are in a slightly better position, they decide to start a family.

In the next year, the output of both their corn and the potatoes enables them to be able to feed themselves and use the surplus to be able to trade for some fertiliser. This leads to a significant improvement in their crop and they now have a sizeable surplus of corn and potatoes. They trade these for a horse, which they use not only for ploughing but also to help fertilise the land.

This story is simple but it does show how the process of wealth creation and economic growth occurs. We can arrive at some conclusions about the factors that help to generate economic growth:

■ the ability to save and invest
■ an enterprising spirit – the willingness to take risks
■ innovation and new product development
■ access to assets – land and capital.

Others factors include:

■ supplies of energy
■ education and training
■ investment in infrastructure – roads, rail, communication networks and so on.

The discovery of new assets, for example, oil or gas reserves or valuable minerals, can change the fortunes of a country. Countries like Venezuela and Nigeria have the potential to become very wealthy because of oil. China's rapid economic growth has been founded on its massive labour force, a highly entrepreneurial spirit and the government's huge investment in new roads, houses and railways.

Investigation

Choose one country that is experiencing strong economic growth – in excess of 5 per cent a year.

1 Investigate the reasons for the rapid growth and identify and explain four key factors that are contributing to the growth.
2 Which of the factors is the most important contributor to the economic growth of the country you have chosen? Explain your reasoning.

22 Growth and resource use

Economic growth involves an increase in the amount of buying and selling that goes on in and between countries through international trade. By definition, it involves larger amounts of output being produced, and this output requires resources.

In China, the rate of economic growth has been very strong for a number of years. In 2006, GDP was estimated to be growing at 10.7 per cent (CIA World Factbook, 2006). There are plans to increase GDP by a further 45 per cent by 2010. Much of the growth in China is in manufactured goods. As the level of output of manufactured goods increases, so does the amount of resources that are needed to produce them.

China has a massive labour force (about 790 million, according to estimates in 2005). Work on the Three Gorges Dam across the Yangtze River is in its final stages. The dam has cost an estimated $24 billion (around £11 billion). It will help to provide large amounts of electricity for the country. In addition to energy resources, China needs huge quantities of extra steel, copper and other metals to build the houses and railways the country needs.

This huge growth in demand for resources resulted in huge, worldwide price rises from 2004 to 2006. China was able to buy increasing proportions of the world's resources because of the wealth generated by its successful exports of manufactured goods.

So, economic growth is associated with increased use of resources.

The expansion of manufacturing in countries like India and China has knock-on effects for the rest of the world. People in the UK can buy cheaper products as a result of this expansion, but there are obvious downsides. As consumers we love cheap imports, but UK workers cannot compete with low-wage workers from developing countries. Once again, we can see that there is an opportunity cost and a trade-off involved.

The increase in China's demand for many different types of raw materials including steel, copper and oil has been rapid. Basic economics will tell us what happens to the prices of these commodities when demand rises faster than the available supply. When the demand for oil or copper or steel rises, it causes a shift in the demand curve to the right. This means that whatever the price, there is now more being demanded. If we assume that capacity levels for these commodities stays the same, then a shortage is created – in other words, demand is greater than the level of available supply. It does not mean that supply cannot be increased – it can, but not in the short term, and only at higher cost.

The result is that prices rise. In some cases, depending on the strength of the rise in demand and the ability of producers to increase supply, the rise in price can be quite significant. These commodities tend to be bought on world markets. That means that traders will buy and sell large quantities of copper, oil and other commodities on behalf of clients – firms in China, for example – that require these raw materials and sources of energy.

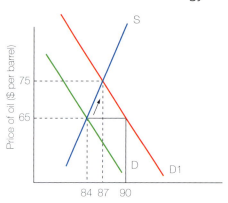

Quantity of oil bought and sold (million barrels per day)

The diagram above shows how we can represent what is happening to the prices of commodities like oil in recent years. The initial price of oil is given as $65 a barrel. At this price, the quantity demanded and supplied is 84 million barrels per day (mbpd).

The increased needs of countries like China and India mean that the demand for oil shifts to the right, indicated by the new demand curve D1. At a price of $65, the demand for oil is now 90 mbpd, but the available supply at that price is still only 84 mbpd. A shortage has developed in the market.

Shortages mean that some buyers of oil are prepared to pay more to get what they need. They are willing to offer higher prices in world oil markets to get the quantity of oil they want. As prices creep higher, suppliers are more willing to find ways of increasing the amount of oil they are producing. It becomes more worthwhile for them to devote additional resources to expanding output because they expect to get a higher price for it. The shortage is gradually reduced as prices creep higher and higher. Eventually, a new equilibrium price and quantity is reached at $75 a barrel, with the amount bought and sold being 87 mbpd.

It is important to remember that this sort of diagram is an attempt to explain what is happening in these types of markets. In reality, of course, the demand for oil is constantly changing and at any time during a day trading of oil on world markets there might be many hundreds of equilibrium positions. Almost as soon as one has been reached, demand or supply will have changed again! This is why markets are referred to as being dynamic.

More trade-offs

In recent years, the price of copper, oil and steel has risen for exactly these reasons. The availability of 'cheap' goods from countries like China is balanced out by the increase in petrol prices that we have had to pay in the UK.

Increasing commodity prices affect us in other ways that we might not immediately appreciate. If you are a football fan or someone who enjoys music and going to concerts, you might have been looking forward to visiting the new Wembley Stadium to watch the FA Cup final in 2006 or go to see Take That, Robbie Williams or Bon Jovi at this wonderful new facility in the summer of 2006. Unfortunately, none of these events took place at Wembley – they had to be moved to other venues. The reason was that the new stadium had not been finished.

One of the reasons it had not been finished was a dispute between the construction company, Multiplex, and one of its sub-contractors over the price of steel. The rising price of steel had led to a dispute between the two and this resulted in a delay over the construction of the steel arch over the stadium.

This example highlights just how interdependent we all are. Interdependent means that one thing depends on another – they are linked in some way. The opportunity cost of ready access to cheaper goods from places like China and India is the sacrifice we have to make in terms of the increased fuel and raw material costs that affect us in other ways.

Economic growth therefore does have to be looked at in terms of the impact it has on resource use. In the next few sections we shall look at other effects of economic growth that might raise questions about how the world is developing and what the consequences and effects of economic growth can be.

Investigation

1 Choose one commodity that is an important raw material or source of energy in fuelling economic growth.
2 Find out what has happened to the price of that commodity in the last five years (give or take a year or so).
3 From your research, identify three causes of the change in the price of that commodity.
4 Which of the factors you have identified do you think is the most important in affecting the change in price of the commodity you have chosen, and why?

23 Can there be more and more?

Sustainable growth

Economic growth is associated with improvements in the standard of living. Economic growth is a good thing, but it does have some problems attached to it. In pushing for more and more economic growth we are putting increased pressure on resources. We know that resources are scarce in relation to the demand for them. Can we afford to continue to keep using up the world's resources to push for more and more economic growth? Can there be more and more?

This depends on a number of things. Many of the resources that are used in production around the world are classed as **non-renewable resources**. This means that there is a limited amount of these resources and if we keep using them then one day they will run out. Oil is a good example of a non-renewable resource. There are still billions of barrels of oil left in known reserves and no doubt there will be more oil found in the future. This new oil, if discovered, is likely to be more expensive to extract and refine. Ultimately, there will be no more oil left worth extracting and at current rates of use it might not be very long before we do run out.

Oil is a non-renewable resource

As we use up resources, the importance of finding different sources of energy and different raw materials becomes more pressing. New energy supplies will be discovered and developed but we will need to combine these new discoveries with other developments. We will need to be aware of the importance of changing our behaviour and the way we look at economic growth.

One way of achieving economic growth but minimising the damage that is being caused to the planet and to natural resources is called **'sustainable growth'**. Sustainable growth refers to economic growth that does not impose a burden on future generations. It looks at ways of generating growth but takes into account the effect of that growth on resources and the effect on the planet. Productivity, innovation and renewable resources are all important factors in helping to move towards sustainable growth.

Productivity

Productivity defined as 'output per person or machine per period of time'. New equipment, machinery and methods can mean that more can be produced using fewer resources.

In 1798, the political economist Robert Malthus wrote his 'Essay on the principle of population'. His thesis was that the world's population was going to grow at a faster rate than the ability to feed them. The end result would be starvation and famine. Such a pessimistic outlook proved to be misguided because Malthus could not foresee the massive improvements in the productivity of land.

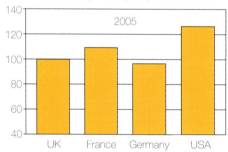

Productivity levels in different countries.
Source: Office for National Statistics

Innovation

One other thing that Malthus did not foresee were the inventions in machinery and techniques that would lead to increases in food production unimagined at that time. Similarly, although people are now very worried about whether the environment is being damaged by economic growth, innovation may still come to the rescue. Sustainable growth needs the world economy to be able to grow without using so much energy. Innovations in insulation, green energy such as solar power and better use of recycling may solve some of the problems. People are very inventive when there is a clear incentive (such as high energy prices).

Renewable resources

The move to find ways of generating economic growth without using up non-renewable resources has led to an increased interest in renewable resources. An important example is renewable energy – solar, wave and wind power, for example – but also energy sources like bio fuels made from crops like wheat, barley and sugar. These types of fuels will become more popular in the years to come and some petrol stations are already selling bioethanol.

Renewable resources also encompass recycling. We need to look at recycling carefully – not all recycling is necessarily 'good'. We need to ask what the cost of recycling is in terms of the resources used and the effects that recycling has on other parts of our lives. If products can be recycled cheaply and with limited effects on society, then it can be a good thing.

Renewable resources also include things like managed forests. Timber is used in many different ways – in construction, manufacturing, furniture, paper manufacturing and so on. The beauty of trees is that they can be regrown. You will see on the inside of some textbooks that the paper they are printed on comes from managed or sustainable forests. This means that for every tree that is cut down at least one new tree is planted to ensure the long-term supply.

Investigation

1 Arrange a visit to a local business to look at sustainability. On your visit, identify the types of resources the business uses and gather some information about its productivity.
2 Prepare a report for the business, evaluating a way in which it might be able to improve its efficiency and/or productivity.

Investigation

Your local council is likely to have a number of recycling schemes.

1 Research the costs to the council of recycling different products.
2 Prepare a report evaluating the efficiency and effectiveness of recycling as a result of your investigation.

24 Externalities

One of the major problems associated with economic growth is the problem of externalities. Externalities are the effects of an economic decision on a **third party**. This means that the effects are felt not only by those involved in a decision but to people, property or organisations that have no involvement in that decision.

For example, if you decide that you wish to smoke you are providing revenue to cigarette companies when you buy them. You and the company are the two parties directly involved in the decision. However, in choosing to smoke you risk increasing the likelihood of damage to your health – the effects are well documented. In addition, if you choose to smoke in a public place you also affect many other people around you. You affect them by inflicting passive smoking on them. Other people who do not smoke breathe in your smoke and run the risk of damaging their health as well. The costs of health treatment for passive smokers are borne by those who do not smoke – the third parties.

Externalities can be classed as either **positive externalities** or **negative externalities**. Positive externalities are the benefits to a third party of a decision. Negative externalities are the costs to a third party of a decision.

Examples of positive externalities:

- An individual decides to have a flu injection. In doing so they reduce the risk of catching flu and then passing it on to someone else.
- A business decides to allow staff to work from home. This reduces congestion on the roads as workers no longer need to use their cars to commute to work.

Examples of negative externalities:

- Noise, air or water pollution from a factory, damaging the environment for local people.

■ Car and aeroplane exhaust fumes, with their impact on carbon levels in the atmosphere and therefore – many believe – impact on global warming.

As economic activity increases, and societies become richer, extra production and consumption may increase the impact of negative externalities. America is already the world's biggest contributor by far to greenhouse gases. Now there are worries that China and India's rapid economic growth will lead them to catch up with the USA's impact on climate change.

It is now widely accepted that all of this activity is leading to climate change. Climate change will lead to the melting of polar ice caps, the raising of sea levels and changes in water temperature. Increases in average temperatures around the world may have harmful effects on wildlife, coastal communities and farmers. Even more serious might be that more and more land in Africa will turn into desert – leading to famine.

In recent years there seem to have been more reports of extremes of weather across the globe – drought, flood, storms, hurricanes, record snowfalls and so on. There are three possible reasons for this:

■ natural changes in weather patterns
■ improved reporting of these kinds of events
■ the impact on the earth of the effects of economic growth.

There is little doubt that the push to increase economic growth generates different externalities, both positive and negative. An important question that we might need to ask is whether the benefits of economic growth are being outweighed by the costs – costs that we may not be experiencing ourselves but may be passing on to future generations.

Investigation

1 Identify three examples of cases of economic growth. Briefly describe the benefits and costs relating to each of your three examples.
2 In each case, which do you think will be the most significant for future generations, the benefits or the costs? Explain your answer.

25 Who should save the planet?

A collective effort

Dealing with the negative effects of economic growth must come from individuals, local government, national government and international governments and bodies. It will have to be a collective effort. There have been a number of attempts to get governments together to look at the problems facing the planet from economic growth. These problems can be summarised as:

- climate change
- impact on water resources
- use of non-renewable resources
- damage to and disappearance of rain forests and wildlife habitats
- extinction of species
- increasing desertification of land
- increases in the number of waste products produced and what to do with the waste.

Some of the problems above are not simply the responsibility of government. There are some that argue that everyone has a responsibility. Simple things like not leaving electrical equipment on standby, for example, could save large amounts of energy in the UK alone. The Energy Saving Trust estimates that around 8 per cent of all domestic energy used goes on standby devices on PCs, TVs, DVD players and so on. This is something that manufacturers of electrical equipment and people who use this equipment – us – have to take responsibility for.

International responsibility

Many argue that the lead must be taken by the international community and that the problems are so serious for future generations that it requires international action. In November 2006, Sir Nicholas Stern, a respected economist, produced a report called 'The Economics of Climate Change'. This report presented a bleak picture about the future of the planet if action is not taken to deal with the impact that economic growth is having.

Sir Nicholas said that the size of the global economy could be reduced by around 20 per cent. The poorest people on the planet, often situated in the most vulnerable countries, would be the ones who would suffer the most from climate change. Drought and flood would be more likely and as a result, over 200 million people could become refugees. Forty per cent of the world's wildlife faces the prospect of extinction as a result of the changes to their natural habitats caused by the effects of climate change.

One of the major attempts to come to terms with the problems posed by climate change has been the Kyoto Protocol. This is an agreement made under the United Nations Framework on Climate Change. The discussions over the treaty began in 1997 in Kyoto, Japan. The difficulties in getting global agreements on reducing greenhouse gases have been considerable. As of December 2006, 169 countries have signed up to the agreement to reduce their emissions of greenhouse gas by 5.2 per cent, compared to the levels that existed in 1990. This might not sound much, but the challenges it presents to the countries that have signed up to it are considerable.

There has been criticism of the Protocol because two key countries have not signed up – Australia and the United States. Both these countries have expressed concern over the effect that the agreement would have on their respective economies and especially on jobs. They also have a problem with the way the treaty has been negotiated. The basis of the discussions was about how we had got to the levels of greenhouse gases that exist today. Countries like the USA, the UK and Europe were part of the first wave of industrialised countries who have been the main contributors to the levels of greenhouse gases we see today. Countries like China and India were exempt from the Kyoto requirements to cut emissions because they had not contributed to current levels. The problem for the USA and Australia is that they believe China and India will soon become the biggest polluters, yet are not being required to cut their emissions.

The Kyoto Protocol finally came into full force in February 2006. Whether it will lead to the reductions in greenhouse gas emissions that countries have agreed upon is yet to be seen. Ultimately, it is individuals who are going to make a difference to the effects of climate change by changing behaviour. To change everyone's behaviour, it is likely that governments both nationally and internationally will need to give a helping hand.

Market failure

The economics of the issue of climate change are simple. We are all consuming goods and services that are provided by businesses. These businesses are creating negative externalities – pollution – which is affecting the climate. The market mechanism is not working properly. This is called **market failure**.

Part of the reason for this market failure is that the prices that people are paying for these goods and services do not reflect the true cost of producing the goods and services. The price we pay might reflect the cost of the land, labour, capital and enterprise that went into providing them but it does not take account of the costs imposed on society – the negative externalities – that are causing the problems.

At the same time, the positive externalities that might come from consumption of certain goods like biofuels or greater use of public transport are not being encouraged. What is needed to correct this market failure, according to Sir Nicholas Stern, is taxation and carbon trading permits.

Possible solutions

Taxing the behaviour that is undesirable aims to make people gradually change their behaviour. If something costs them more to buy, then they might think more carefully about consuming it. Carbon trading permits are licences to emit a certain amount of carbon per year. To work properly, they need to be set at limits that are below what are currently being emitted. If a business is able to find ways of making itself more efficient and reducing its carbon emissions, it can sell any excess permit to other firms who might not have been able to afford or implement the necessary efficiencies.

In the UK there are plans to begin pilot schemes to assess the effectiveness of road pricing. Road users would have to pay to use the roads. Any such system might mean the driver having to pay up to £1.30 per mile if they travel at peak times. The EU has introduced a carbon trading scheme. Both types of strategy might start the process of making individuals, businesses and governments more aware of the problems they are storing up for future generations. It is yet to be seen whether such measures will work to a level that makes a long-term difference to behaviour and to the reduction of negative externalities and boosting of positive externalities.

Investigation

1 Find out the level of emissions of greenhouse gases of the major countries in the developing world. (United Nations Framework Convention on Climate Change at: http://unfccc.int/2860.php) Is there any evidence that emissions of greenhouse gases are falling?

2 Australia argues that if it closed all its coal-fired power stations today, within a year China would have produced more than enough pollution to take its place. To what extent is this argument justified as a means of Australia refusing to sign the Kyoto Protocol?

26 Stakeholder rights and responsibilities

A stakeholder is any individual, group or organisation that has an interest in the success of a business. The main stakeholders in a business are:

- employees
- managers
- shareholders
- the local community
- suppliers
- customers
- the government.

Each of these stakeholders may have an interest for a different reason. An employee, for example, will be interested in the extent to which they have job security (whether they will have a job in the long term), the terms and conditions under which they are employed, the amount of holidays and benefits they get from their work, and also the wages or salary they receive.

Shareholders may be looking for other things. For example, they will hope that the share price will rise and that profit levels will be high because that might mean better dividends. (A dividend is a share of the profits given to shareholders.)

These two things may well come into conflict with each other. Higher wages for workers means higher costs for the business and this might affect profits – not what shareholders might be looking for! Many businesses therefore have problems in meeting the needs of all stakeholders because of these conflicts. Businesses will be looking to find ways in which they can balance all the competing demands of stakeholders on the business – not an easy thing to do.

Below is a summary of the rights and responsibilities of the different stakeholders that we have identified.

Stakeholder	Right	Responsibility
Employee	■ To receive a reasonable wage ■ To have access to employee rights guaranteed in law ■ To have standards of health and safety at work	■ To honour the contract of employment they have been given ■ To abide by the rules and regulations of the business ■ To do the job they are being paid for to the best of their ability
Shareholder	■ To have a say in the running of the business ■ To expect high quality and honest information from the business ■ To receive a share in the profits	■ To provide capital for the business ■ To take an interest in the running of the business when appropriate
Government	■ To receive taxes due ■ To expect the business to abide by the laws of the land ■ To complete paperwork and administration to provide information when requested	■ To offer advice and provide accurate and timely information relating to the laws of the land and regulations that the government may pass ■ To make the tax system for businesses as fair and simple to understand and administer as possible
Supplier	■ To receive payment for goods supplied in line with agreed terms and conditions	■ To provide goods and services on time and of a suitable quality within the terms of the agreed contract
Local community	■ To have the business abide by laws and regulations that are designed to protect them	■ To enable the business to carry out its legitimate business activity without undue interference
Customers	■ To expect goods and services of appropriate quality at appropriate prices ■ To expect to be protected from dangerous products and services	■ To pay the business for the good or service purchased within an accepted time frame ■ To abide by the laws and rules set up by the authorities in relation to business law (i.e. not expect to get replacements for goods that have been damaged in use; and to abide by copyright law)
Managers	■ To expect to be paid a reasonable salary for the work done	■ To run the business for the benefit of the shareholders ■ To keep the shareholders informed of the performance of the business ■ To meet the statutory and regulatory responsibilities of the business

In attempting to balance out stakeholder rights and responsibilities there are no right answers. Each business will have to find a balance that they think works for them. For example, a business may need to persuade its shareholders that a rise in pay levels matched by increases in productivity would enable the business to be more efficient – total costs might increase, but if productivity rises at a faster rate than wages, the average costs would be less. This could allow the business to improve profit margins, and if sales were maintained or improved, then profit would ultimately increase.

The business may have to look at both the short-term and the long-term effects of decisions that it makes with regard to balancing stakeholder rights and responsibilities. The business may need to work hard to think through its decisions and to consider what effect it will have on its stakeholders. In doing so, it can try to adjust its decisions in the light of these effects. The argument that it puts forward must then not only be supported by data, but in the long term must produce the desired results.

Investigation

Christmas 2006 was a difficult time for thousands of families across the UK. These families had taken part in a savings scheme with a company called Farepak. The families saved money during the year through agents who collected the money from them. The plan was that in December, the families would receive vouchers for various stores to enable them to buy Christmas gifts and food, thereby spreading the cost of Christmas and avoiding going into debt at an expensive time of the year.

Farepak was owned by a company called European Homes Retail (EHR) which had been in some financial difficulties but were supported by their bank, Halifax Bank of Scotland (HBOS). HBOS extended the overdraft that EHR had to give them time to sort out their problems. In October it became obvious to HBOS that things were getting worse and so they refused to extend the overdraft any further. EHR closed down and Farepak also ceased trading. The families lost over £60 million in savings. The average lost by each family was around £600. Agents lost their jobs. HBOS recovered around £29 million of the debt that it was owed.

Members of the government were highly critical of the role of HBOS in the Farepak incident. They called in HBOS, who had made £4.8 billion profit in 2005, to help the families and also explain why they had continued to allow the families to go on saving with the scheme when they knew of the financial difficulties that EHR had.

Some companies like Tesco and Sainsbury offered some money to a fund set up to help the families; members of parliament were encouraged to give up a day's pay to contribute to the fund and HBOS itself contributed £2 million. The fund eventually ended up at around £6 million. Families got some help, but nothing like the amount they had lost .

HBOS said that it was 'very comfortable' with how it handled the whole affair. It had a responsibility to EHR and did everything it could to support the company through its difficulties. Ultimately, it argued, it had a responsibility to its customers and shareholders to conduct its business properly. Its customer was EHR, not Farepak.

■ Consider the various stakeholder rights and responsibilities in this story. To what extent do you think that HBOS was right in 'feeling comfortable' with its decisions in this case?

27 How should companies behave?

Do you believe that testing cosmetic products on animals is wrong? How about testing potentially life-saving drugs for humans on monkeys? Should a business pay a fair sum of money to suppliers and growers of products in less developed countries? Should a business be responsible for the waste products that it produces?

All these are questions associated with what we might class as being a 'right' or a 'wrong' way to act. Business activity has effects that are felt by immediate stakeholders such as customers, shareholders and employees. The effects may also be far-reaching for society as a whole – and even the planet.

Ethics in business

Given these effects, how should a business behave? This is the focus of corporate responsibility and **ethics**. Ethics relates to what is right and wrong. An ethical decision by a business is one that is taken for the 'right' reasons. The difficulty is defining what is 'right'.

In general, we might say that the right decision is the one that most people would agree is an appropriate way of behaving. Or perhaps a course of action that benefits as many people as possible and reduces the costs or negative effects to a minimum.

Every day in every office there are ethical questions to be tackled.

Some seem trivial, such as whether it is acceptable to pocket a couple of pens to use at home. But isn't that stealing? Others are more serious, such as whether a business decision has been influenced by bribery. A manager may have the power to give an £80,000 contract to a particular supplier. Is it acceptable for the manager to accept two tickets to Bermuda from the supplier? Surely not. But what about a slap-up lunch at Gordon Ramsey's 3-star restaurant in London? Most managers would happily accept this expensive 'thank-you'.

Far more important than these issues of personal ethics are questions about the ethics of the business. Can it be ethically justifiable for a cigarette company to even exist? Should shareholders in tobacco companies happily accept and spend their dividend pay-outs? In every company, there are many important ethical questions. These may affect their sales and marketing, their production and delivery systems and how they treat their staff.

Ethical issues within sales and marketing:

- How can **Marks & Spencer** justify putting sweets, chocolates and crisps at every cash desk? This is purely to encourage people to impulse-buy more of these items than they intended to. Isn't Marks & Spencer an ethical company?
- In January 2007 a new, independent supermarket owned by Mr Delves was to open in Ludlow, Shropshire. Just beforehand, **Tesco** sent leaflets to households within a 10-mile radius of Ludlow offering them £10 off for every £30 spent in the Ludlow Tesco. Mr Delves accused Tesco of 'predatory pricing' (meaning trying to put him out of business). Tesco denies this, but it still raises questions about the ethics of how the supermarket giant Tesco deals with small competitors.

Ethical issues within production and delivery:

- Workforce safety should be seen by managers as an ethical duty. Some firms cut corners, which cannot be justified if it is simply to boost profits.
- Tesco on-line has been a great success; but is it justifiable environmentally to provide door-to-door delivery of groceries? At the very least, shouldn't Tesco's delivery vehicles all be electric-powered?

Ethical issues relating to staff:

- In recent years, many large companies have insisted on low pay settlements for staff (such as a 2.5 per cent pay rise) while the directors have given themselves rises of 20 per cent or more. This is unethical if directors are simply taking advantage of their own power.
- In the City of London, several women have taken their banking employers to court for sex discrimination – and won. Firms have an ethical duty to be fair to all their staff

Social responsibilities

The extent of these issues is massive. **BP**, the oil producer, had to deal with an explosion at a refinery in Texas which led to the loss of 15 lives and 180 injured and leakages in some of its pipelines in Alaska. Every business should think carefully about the health and safety of its workers – even though this adds to its costs.

The railway industry in the UK has had to grapple with problems with signalling and track maintenance that has led to a number of crashes, again leading to loss of life.

Each of these examples suggests that a firm might be able to influence outcomes as a result of its behaviour, and is responsible for its actions. Many businesses are now taking corporate social responsibility (CSR) more seriously.

Some are producing reports on their CSR each year. These reports are designed to tell the public what the business has done to try and minimise the impact of its actions on the environment. It might be that they have adopted widespread homeworking schemes for its employees to help reduce the use of cars and fuel. It might introduce policies to cut down on the use of paper, improve the safety awareness of its staff, provide crèches to help mothers with young children return to work and so on.

> **Good Company Limited**
> **Corporate Social**
> **Responsibility Report**
> **2007**
>
>
> Prepared for Good
> Company Limited by
> Clever Consultants

There may be very good business reasons why a business might choose to publicise its attempts to behave in a more responsible way. It may believe that this is what its customers want. Changing its behaviour to reflect this is simply anticipating and responding to customer needs – in other words, good marketing. Of course, if the attempt to gain favourable publicity leads to better behaviour by firms, no one should complain. However, there is a concern that some large firms have spent a lot of money publicising their CSR policies, while neglecting their real safety responsibilities. A business may genuinely believe it has responsibilities, but for others the main focus of their CSR may be competitive advantage – a means of trying to get more sales.

Whatever the reason, CSR is increasingly seen as important. There appears to be a widespread belief that the benefits that businesses bring have a price – the effects on society. Behaving responsibly and ethically has taken centre stage. In part, this has been due to the greater availability of information, to the activities of pressure groups and to a realisation that business activity has far-reaching effects on things like climate change – far more so than we might previously have believed. One of the problems of a firm taking more positive action on issues of concern and spending money on changing its behaviour is that it affects their costs. Are you, as a customer, prepared to pay more for your goods and services as a result? The responsibility for actions therefore does not just stop with the business.

If business behaviour can be changed to reduce negative externalities and promote positive externalities then this is something that most people would welcome.

All of the following are possible titles that can lead you on an extensive investigation. There are, of course, plenty of other things that you can look at. You may decide to choose one area or you may use these as the basis of class discussion to explore the issues surrounding CSR.

Investigation

1 To what extent should McDonalds and other fast food restaurants be responsible for the litter that they produce?
2 Should supermarkets charge for shopping bags?
3 To what extent should firms providing fast food be held responsible for the rise in obesity levels in the developed world?
4 Should we all buy Fairtrade food products?
5 If safety on airlines and on the railways is important, should firms in the industry invest whatever it takes to make our journeys as safe as they can be?
6 Is it ever right to conduct experiments on animals to develop products for humans?

28 External pressure and business behaviour

Businesses and governments make many decisions in the course of their daily activities. Not everyone agrees with these decisions. For example, I might disagree with plans to open a new supermarket in my local town. What can I do if I disagree with this decision? I could try and write to the supermarket and my local council and present my views and argument. I might not get very far on my own, however. If there are other people in my area that think in the same way then it may be beneficial to join together. A group of people are more likely to be listened to rather than an individual. Then the supermarket and the local council may start to listen.

This is the basis behind the development of **pressure groups**. Pressure groups represent the views and beliefs of people or organisations with the aim of changing business behaviour or government policy. Pressure groups exist in a wide range of different areas. They represent a range of different views and opinions and adopt a variety of strategies to make their point and get behaviour changed. Well-known pressure groups include **Greenpeace** and **Friends of the Earth**.

Pressure groups use many different ways to get their message across, such as:

- lobbying a member of parliament or the government (this means contacting MPs and the government to present your view and offer suggestions for changes to policies and laws)
- encouraging people not to use the products or services of a business that you think is not operating as you would like (known as 'boycotting')
- publishing research and statistics to support your case
- organising demonstrations and protest marches
- direct action – perhaps including illegal acts (such as breaking into a laboratory and releasing the animals, if you oppose animal testing)
- organising petitions.

Many of these activities might not be just one-offs, they might involve persistent action over a long period of time. Groups like Greenpeace and Friends of the Earth have become very large organisations in their own right but began as a small group of like-minded people. In other cases, a pressure group might form to campaign against a specific thing (such as the opening of a new supermarket). Once the action has been won (or lost) the group no longer needs to exist.

Should businesses take notice of pressure groups? The answer to that depends on many factors, including:

■ the nature of the view being put forward by the pressure group: does the group have a real case (such as the group Lynx, with its anti-fur message)?
■ the size of the business: it may be very hard for a household name such as Marks & Spencer to resist an attack on its public image
■ whether the protest is based on evidence: there have been cases where claims of fact by a pressure group have later been proven to be wrong.

The **tobacco industry** faced a dilemma in responding to pressure groups about its behaviour. For many years, tobacco companies allegedly withheld information from the public about the danger to health of smoking. Smoking was even promoted as being something that was a 'good' thing – that it helped smokers relax and was a social thing to do. However, as the weight of the evidence accumulated, tobacco companies were forced to change the way they operated. In some cases, they responded to pressure group activity, such as agreeing to stop advertising cigarettes on TV. Later, it required changes in the law to ban cigarette advertising completely.

Pressure groups therefore can be very successful in getting policies and laws changed and decisions influenced. In many cases, it does depend on the strength of the case being put forward by the pressure group and how widely the group can get its message across. It would be rather pointless, for example, for a tobacco company to try and claim that smoking was 'good', given the weight of the evidence that exists to the contrary.

There might be concerns, however, about how far pressure groups should go to make their point. Is illegal action ever justified, or should pressure groups always operate inside the law? Some might argue that some things are so important that mere petitions or protests alone are not enough to change decisions in large organisations. They argue that these organisations are so big that they almost believe they are above the law, and it needs extreme measures to make the public aware of what is really going on and why things need to change.

Investigation

1 Identify a pressure group – it could be a large organisation or a smaller local group that you are aware of.
2 Explain what their views are about the issue they are concerned with, and what they want done about it.
3 To what extent do you think that businesses or government will change their behaviour as a result of the activities of the pressure group?

SECTION 5

WINNERS AND LOSERS

29 The effects of inequality

What do we mean by inequality?

The GDP in the UK has risen steadily since 1971. This would imply that the country is richer than it was in 1971. But does that mean everyone is better off? Not necessarily. There may have been an increase in inequality – rich people getting richer while poorer people get poorer.

It is important to understand the difference between **income** and **wealth**.

Income refers to a flow of money over a period of time. For example, someone might earn £300 per week, or have a salary of £25,000 a year. Some people receive an income through a pension, rents from a property or interest from savings. The level of income is one factor in determining inequalities between countries. The GDP of a country tells us the value of output in a country over a year. If we divide that figure by the number of people in the country (the population) we get a figure called **GDP per capita**. This gives a measure of the average income. Individual people within that country may earn much more than the average, and many others will earn much less.

Wealth is a stock of assets at a point in time. A person's assets are all the things that the person owns. This might be in the form of property, cars, shares, land, and personal assets like TVs, other household goods and so on. A person might be very wealthy but have a relatively small income. For example, some people own large properties like stately

homes but they do not have very large incomes. One of the main causes of inequalities in the UK is the extent to which wealth is passed down from one person to another – inheritance. In the UK this is an important source of inequality.

One per cent of the UK population owns 21 per cent of the wealth of the country – that means there is a small number of very wealthy people.

Inequality refers to one or both of the key differences between rich and poor – inequalities of income or of wealth. Within this country, wealth inequalities can be attributed to:

- family – some people have been lucky enough to inherit a large sum or a large house from a wealthy relative
- enterprise – some have built up their own fortune through their clever business sense, or their intelligent (or lucky) investments (e.g. in stocks and shares).

When looking at any definition of inequality we have to think about the terms that we are using. In most developed countries, including the UK, there are significant differences between the very rich in society and the very poor. This is largely due to the distribution of wealth – who owns what.

There are also important differences in the incomes earned by different people. This is largely down to:

- education – research has shown that the average university graduate earns £150,000 more over their lifetime than those who have not been to university
- personal qualities and skills – bright and hard-working staff are likely to achieve success even if they started at the bottom
- luck or connections – there is no doubt that family connections can help enormously in getting started in some of the most attractive or well-paid jobs.

We can look at inequality at a number of different levels.

Individual inequality

This occurs where there are differences in incomes or wealth between individuals. The Prime Minister's salary in the UK in 2006 was about £187,600: an experienced teacher would have earned about £30,000.

This table shows changes in the average income per week over a period of time. The poorest 10 per cent of the population earned around £100 per week in 1971 and by 2002/03 this had risen to an average of around £175 per week. By contrast, the top 10 per cent of earners (the '90th percentile') earned around £320 per week in 1970 and this had risen to about £650 per week by 2002/03. When the gap between these two gets bigger, it means income inequalities are getting greater.

£ per week at 2002/03 prices

90th percentile

Median

10th percentile

1971   1977   1983   1989   1995/96   2002/03

Regional inequality

This occurs where there are differences in incomes and wealth within regions of a country. The East End of London includes areas such as Canary Wharf and also places like Barking and Canning Town. The wealth of people who live in and around Canary Wharf and the value of the properties in this area are different to that in places like Canning Town, which is a relatively deprived area.

National and international inequality

National inequality occurs where there are differences in incomes and wealth between regions of a country. Cornwall, for example, has a lower average income per head of the population in that county compared to Surrey. The value of properties in Cornwall tends not to be as high as that of the properties in Surrey.

Some countries are very much richer than others – the wealth of the USA and the average income per head of the population is significantly higher than that of Sierra Leone. In the USA, the average income per head in 2006 was equivalent to around £22,900, whereas in Sierra Leone it was just £470. (Source: CIA World Factbook.)

Income distribution

Income distribution refers to the proportion of income paid to different people in a country. Imagine that a country consists of 100 people and its total income is £100,000 a year. If income was distributed equally, then each person would be earning £1,000 per year. However, let us assume that ten people in this country each earn £5,000 a year and the remaining 90 earn just over £555 a year. In this case, income is distributed unequally. Ten people are relatively rich compared to the remaining 90.

We could have a situation where ten people earn £5,000 per year, 80 earn £612.50 per year and the remaining ten earn just £100 per year. In this case, the bottom 10 per cent earns just 1 per cent of the total income of the country. The top 10 per cent earn 50 per cent of the income of the country.

This is how we look at income distribution – by looking at the proportion of the total income earned by different proportions of the population. This gives us an indication of the extent of inequalities in a country and a means of comparisons between different countries.

Wealth distribution would be looked at in a similar way, but by measuring ownership of assets rather than incomes. As a general rule, wealth distribution is more unequal than income distribution.

Some countries appear to be very 'rich' – Brazil, for example, is by GDP terms a rich country. It is the ninth biggest economy in the world. In 2005, its GDP was estimated at $1.536 trillion. You might think that this would indicate that the population of Brazil was relatively well off. In reality there are around a quarter of the population living below the poverty line. The top 10 per cent of the population, however, own over 30 per cent of the wealth of the country. (Source: CIA Factbook.)

Many of the terms in this section, such as 'rich' and 'poor' are 'relative terms'. These are terms that only really make sense when you relate them to something else. If you live in a developed country like the UK, you may not describe yourself as 'rich'. However, many families in Africa would describe your family as 'rich' because you have some material goods and other advantages (such as access to food, clothes and education) that they do not have.

The significance of inequality

One of the most important factors influencing human behaviour is the difference between the 'haves' and the 'have-nots'. When one group of people have more than another, there is always the potential for problems to arise. The more extreme the inequalities, the more likely it is that there will be problems. Many of the world's conflict zones and trouble spots have economic problems as the real root cause. With inequality comes accusations of unfairness and it is this that leads to conflict.

If you look at the history of the UK, rioting and tension in towns and cities has taken place many times. The cause is often that one group of people see that others are being treated better than they are. It may be that some groups have better access to jobs, government benefits, housing or other support.

In the Middle East, there are political problems with access to land. Linked to this is the fact that the Palestinian people have to live in very difficult conditions. The quality of housing, water and electricity is very poor. Unemployment is high and wages for those who are employed are low. Many Palestinians believe that the cause of their unequal status and their economic difficulties is due to Israel. The Israelis have quite a different opinion.

There is no argument, though, that many world problems can be traced to problems of inequality. It is, therefore, a very important factor to consider in any economic analysis.

Investigation

1 Find some data on income distribution in the UK, using the Office for National Statistics. The annually published 'Social Trends' by the ONS is a useful source of information.
2 Find out what has been happening to either:
- income distribution in the UK
- regional data about inequalities.
3 To what extent has the degree of inequality in your chosen area increased in the last ten years? Explain your answer.

Investigation

1 Choose one country and do some research to find out how its GDP and GDP per capita and income distribution have changed in the last five years.
2 Describe the changes to the data identified over the time period chosen.
3 To what extent has the country reduced income and wealth inequalities over the time period selected? Explain your answer.

Useful websites

CIA World Factbook
https://www.cia.gov/cia/publications/factbook/index.html
The World Bank
www.worldbank.org
The ONS
www.statistics.gov.uk
The Organisation for Economic Cooperation and Development (OECD)
www.oecd.org
United Nations statistics division
http://unstats.un.org/unsd/default.htm
EU statistics
www.eustatistics.gov.uk

30 The meaning of poverty

Poverty is another term that is relative. There are two key definitions of poverty that we need to identify. **Absolute poverty** refers to a situation where individuals do not have sufficient income to afford or gain access to the basics for existence in life, things such as food, clothing and shelter. **Relative poverty** refers to a situation of a family that is unable to buy the things that are considered part of normal life for people in that society. For example, some pensioners in the UK have a home and enough food, but may not have enough money to be able to go out. People in relative poverty are not able to take a full part in society in the same way that other people can.

These two definitions help us compare how people live in different countries. Someone who is considered 'poor' in the UK might not be considered 'poor' compared to a refugee living in a country like Sudan. The Sudanese person may have to live in a tent and have limited access to food and water. By comparison, the person in the UK might have a flat, income support from the government and access to food, clothing, electricity and water.

The difference in the standard of living of these two people is clear. In the case of the UK example, the person may have an income that is much lower than the national average. They may consider themselves poor because they are unable to afford a holiday or a car. The person in the Sudan may suffer from hunger and thirst and live in very basic accommodation. The extent of their poverty differs considerably.

How do we define poverty?

The fact that poverty is a relative term means that it is often difficult to arrive at a clear definition of what poverty means in practice. The charity **Oxfam** reports that one in every four people in the UK (that amounts to around 13 million people) live in poverty. The figures for children living in poverty are also startling. One in three children (around 4 million) live in poverty.

In a country like the UK, a person is said to be living in poverty if they earn less than 60 per cent of the median income. The median is the middle value of a set of data – in this case income. This measure is often used because it takes into account the range of incomes that exist in a country. The Institute for Fiscal Studies (IFS) suggested that the median income in 2006 in the UK was £17,742. Using the 60 per cent measure, this means that an adult person who earned less than £10,645 was said to be living in poverty. This definition of poverty has now been widely accepted as a standard measure. It is used in the European Union and by the United Nations.

For people in the UK who live in poverty, what does this mean? Oxfam reports that around 6.5 million people go without what they refer to as 'essential clothing' such as a warm waterproof winter coat because they cannot afford to buy one. And 9.5 million people cannot afford to live in homes that are heated adequately or free from damp. Some families report not being able to afford some basic food items on a regular basis.

Children in poverty may not have access to toys, appropriate clothing or even to three meals a day. Their life expectancy is lower and there is a higher infant mortality rate among children in poverty. The **infant mortality rate** is the number of children dying in the first year of life as a proportion of 1,000 live births.

In the UK, the infant mortality rate is around five. In a country like India it is around 56 and in Angola it is 187. Children born into poverty are also more likely to suffer from ill health, have a greater likelihood of not benefiting from educational opportunities, and a higher risk of being unemployed when they become adults.

What causes poverty?

Slipping into poverty can be all too easy. People can be born into poverty and find it very difficult to escape. Employment is the main way in which people can escape poverty. Yet even if an individual is able to get a job it does not mean that the income they earn is sufficient to get them out of poverty. There are many causes of poverty.

Not having a job

This is the root cause of many people living in poverty. Not having a job invariably means that a person's income is much less than would be the case if they had paid work. Not having a job can be caused by not having the appropriate qualifications or skills, being made redundant, not being able to afford housing in areas where jobs might be available, ill health, disability and so on.

Ill health or disability

Some people might suffer from long-term ill health which prevents them from working. As a result they have to survive on state benefits which tend to be very much lower than incomes that can be earned through employment.

Being over 65

Many of the UK's poorest individuals are those over the age of 65. This group of people may have retired from work and rely on the state pension for their income. The state pension in the UK as at April 2006 was £84.25 per week for a single person and £134.75 for a couple. This represents an annual income of £4,381 for a single person and £7,007 for a couple, which is well below the 60 per cent of median income for the UK. In many other countries where the state does not have such support mechanisms in place, things are even worse for older people.

Poor mental health

Poor mental health may mean that a person is unable to secure a job but might also mean that they need ongoing treatment or care. Many people who have a mental illness might have to survive on state benefits and this tends to mean an income level that is less than 60 per cent of median income.

War

In many developing countries war has led to people being displaced from their homes. They might end up being refugees many miles from home and even in different countries. In such circumstances, poverty is a real prospect.

Disease

Disease not only affects the person who is ill but also the other members of the family. In the developing world, HIV/Aids, malaria and tuberculosis are major sources of poverty. Such diseases can kill income-earning members of the family and many children are left orphaned and destined for lives in poverty. In many of these countries, the support mechanisms to help people caught in this type of situation either does not exist or is too stretched to be able to cope.

Drought

In many developing countries, drought causes harvests to fail. When harvests fail, not only might there be insufficient food to feed people but there is a lack of quality seed for sowing for the next year. In some parts of Africa, repeated droughts have caused year-on-year problems that eventually lead to famine.

Political problems

Some countries may suffer from poverty because of the actions of their political leaders. Leaders may spend money on their own personal projects at the expense of their people. In addition, many poor countries suffer from corruption among government officials. This makes it difficult for business to flourish and to attract investment from abroad. Inevitably, it is the most vulnerable that tend to suffer as a result.

Investigation

1 Identify a country with a relatively large proportion of its population living in poverty.
2 Do some research to identify the main causes of the poverty in that country. Use the causes given above as the basis for helping you with this. Explain how each of the factors you have identified contribute to the poverty that the country experiences.
3 Of the factors you have identified, which is the most significant cause of poverty in the country and why?

Investigation

1 Select two countries that are quite different in terms of their GDP or GDP per capita.
2 Find out what the income distribution is in the two countries.
3 Analyse the causes of the differences/similarities in the income distribution of the two countries. To what extent does this help to explain the incidence of poverty in these two countries?

31 Charities and NGOs

Many governments in poor countries do try to take positive action to tackle the problems of poverty in their countries – some with more vigour than others. International efforts to help reduce poverty are also common. There are a number of international institutions that do extensive work in relieving the effects of poverty. They also try to put strategies in place to combat the causes of poverty.

However, in many cases, relief work for those affected by poverty is carried out by organisations that are nothing to do with a government. There are a number of charities that exist that seek to help those affected by poverty. Some of these charities help those in poverty in the UK. Others will have a presence in many countries.

These charities are often very large organisations in their own right. They raise massive sums of money every year and have many different projects that they are involved with. **Oxfam**, for example, has a global spend of £250 million each year, while **Comic Relief** has raised over £425 million since it was first started in 1985.

Non-governmental organisations (NGOs)

The World Bank defines NGOs as 'private organisations that pursue activities to relieve suffering, promote the interests of the poor, protect the environment, provide basic social services or undertake community development'.

The vast majority of NGOs are non-profit-making organisations, and some have charitable status. Examples include:

- CARE International
- Center for Sustainable Development
- International Agency for Economic Development
- Overseas Development Institute
- Resource Africa
- Save the Children

- Action Aid
- International Federation Red Cross and Red Crescent Societies
- Oxfam.

The work of these organisations is extensive. Whenever there are disasters around the world, famine, drought, conflict and just plain simple problems of poverty, charities and NGOs are there to help. They are often the first organisations to reach scenes of difficulty and many have on-going operations in many of the world's poorest countries.

They help provide short-term help, such as food, water, clothing and shelter. They also engage in education and health campaigns and programmes, providing the means by which communities can access water and other resources. They try to help people to help themselves. Some will also help women to take a fuller part in society – to get education and equal rights with men.

How one NGO worked with governments to help combat drought

Prolonged droughts have caused difficulties for the people in northern Kenya. Many people in this area rely on herding animals for their livelihood. They may travel hundreds of miles in searching for food and water for their animals.

Much of Kenya is subject to frequent droughts, which occur every three or four years. With only 200–300mm of rain every year, people in northern Kenya have learned over the centuries to cope in this dry environment and respect the resources they have. However, due to more frequent droughts, refugee

movements and population growth, this way of life has come under increased stress.

One of the most common responses to these problems has been to develop new water points to ensure that people have adequate water supplies throughout the year for both their own and their livestock's use. Although well intentioned, these efforts have sometimes caused even more problems. Settlements tend to be built around these permanent water sources. The trees are cut for firewood and the pasture is overgrazed by the resident and visiting camels, cows, goats and

sheep. A once-healthy environment becomes a soil-depleted wasteland. The populations of these new settlements are often more vulnerable to drought periods than before, relying on relief food and assistance in these difficult times.

With funding support from the European Commission, **Oxfam-Quebec** teamed up with local governments and other groups to employ the latest Geographic Information Systems (GIS) technology for tackling these planning challenges. The team has so far surveyed over 1,500 water points in

Mandera, Wajir and Marsabit. This year, local staff in each district will be rigorously trained to update and utilise the database for district-level planning.

Water resource mapping therefore gives district planners an invaluable tool for thoroughly evaluating the most promising sites for developing water points and assessing existing ones. This becomes instrumental in managing the drought cycle in these northern regions. With more information available to them, district and national level decision-makers will be able to plan more efficiently for prolonged dry periods and reduce the impacts of drought to farming communities.

(Source: Adapted from www.oxfam.org/en/programs/ development/ceafrica/kenya_ water.htm)

Investigation

1 Choose a charity that aims to try and help deal with poverty, either in the UK or elsewhere in the world.

2 What projects does it help to fund and how do these projects aim to help relieve poverty?

3 Assess the success of the work of this charity in relieving poverty through the projects you have investigated.

32 The role of government in poverty

Poverty in the UK

Tackling poverty is a challenging task. UK and other national governments provide many programmes and funding to help tackle poverty. Governments use the tax and benefits system as the main means of doing this. People who live in poverty may not have to pay any income tax or get tax credits to help them. People who are living in poverty can get help through various benefits such as:

- disability allowances
- winter fuel payments for elderly people
- help for those caring for others
- support for people who are not able to work because of illness
- housing benefit, Council Tax benefit and many other forms of help and support.

The Labour Government, which was elected in 1997 has made tackling child poverty a key part of its programme. It has set a target of eradicating child poverty by 2020. It has outlined a variety of ways in which the number of children who live in poverty can be helped. This includes:

- helping people find work – with incomes families can move out of poverty
- offering increased help for those who cannot work because of illness or disability
- improving public services that have a role to play in helping children escape from poverty – this includes improving educational opportunities, health services and helping local councils deal with housing and deprived environments.

The targets the government has set are challenging. In 2005 the Chancellor of the Exchequer said that the programme had helped 2 million children out of poverty. Raising Child Tax Credit for the poorest families was one important factor in this success according to the government. Child Tax Credit is a payment for people with children. It is heavily weighted in favour of those who are on lower incomes. For example, in 2005–2006, a family with three children and a joint income of £50,000 could claim £545 a year in Child Tax Credit. By contrast, a family with three children and a joint income of between £5,000 and £10,000 a year could claim £5,625 a year.

Dealing with international poverty is a different matter. Many poor countries do not have the resources or tax revenue to offer the sort of support that the UK government can provide. In these cases, the poverty of the country makes it very difficult to solve the problems of the poorest in the society.

Poverty in other countries

We have seen that poverty is a relative term. What is considered poverty in the UK would not necessarily be viewed as a problem in many other countries.

Do richer countries do enough to help poorer ones? One of the main factors that could reduce in poverty in less-developed countries is to help improve trade between countries. Many poor countries have difficulties selling their goods to richer countries because of some barrier to trade – taxes or subsidies, for example. This means they are unable to generate wealth and escape from poverty. Many of the countries that talk about helping the less well-off, in fact make it harder for the poorer countries to help themselves. America, Britain and the European Union as a whole have all been accused of this.

There are a number of international organisations that were set up to tackle world poverty and to help poor countries to trade with the rich ones.

The World Bank

The World Bank offers support for middle-income countries and countries that might be poor but who are considered 'creditworthy'. In other words, they can be trusted with loans and financial support. It also exists to help the very poorest countries in the world. To the poorest countries, the World Bank provides low-interest loans. This is to encourage them to invest in health, education and communications and thereby tackle poverty and promote economic development. However, there are many critics of the World Bank who believe that their actions are not always helpful. These include the World Bank's former Chief Economist, Joseph Stiglitz. He feels that the World Bank forces poorer countries to take actions that may be damaging to the poorest in the community, such as privatising water supply.

The World Bank

The World Trade Organisation (WTO)

The WTO deals with the global rules governing trade between nations. It monitors trade between nations and draws up international agreements on trade. If there are disputes between countries about trade issues, it acts as an intermediary to help settle them. At the heart of its work is the attempt to get agreement between nations to reduce trade barriers and enable all countries to gain the benefits of trade.

The WTO has been engaged in major talks for a number of years in attempts to get trade barriers reduced and freeing up the world's trading system. These talks have not been easy. There are 149 members of the WTO, with another 32 classed as observers. The number of countries and the different requirements and problems they all have make the task of the WTO especially difficult. Most members realise the importance of advancing trade negotiations but equally understand the domestic pressures they are under to secure favourable agreements for their own people.

The United Nations

The United Nations Department of Economic and Social Affairs (UNDESA) has a key role to play within the UN movement. The UN devotes around 70 per cent of its work to trying to improve standards of living, improving welfare and reducing poverty. The UNDESA carries out work in three main areas.

- It compiles information about economic, social and environmental conditions throughout the world to help member states in decision-making.
- It brings together member states and intergovernmental groups to help make decisions on key problems and issues.
- It provides advice to countries on how they can put into practice UN policies and provide practical assistance in such tasks.

Investigation

Investigate the proposition that the UK government should focus its attention on dealing with poverty in the UK and not on projects abroad. Evaluate the economic arguments for and against such a statement.

Investigation

Do some research into the work of either the WTO or the World Bank. Choose one of the projects that either organisation has focused on in recent years and write an evaluation of the success of the project concerned.

33 Why trade? Benefits and costs

How trade works

One of the most important factors that can contribute to the fall in poverty levels in countries is the development of trade. Trade refers to the exchange of one good or service for another. Trade developed because individuals were able to generate surpluses of goods – items they did not need to survive. Then they used these to buy things that they could not produce or did not have access to. In early cases of trade, items were exchanged for each other at some mutually agreeable rate of exchange.

For example, in South America, the Aztecs seemed to have an endless supply of gold. It did not appear to have the scarcity value that it had in Western Europe. Early traders negotiated rates of exchange between them at a mutually acceptable rate. One horse, for example, might have a value of ten pieces of gold. Both sides will have felt that they were getting a good deal, otherwise the deal would not go ahead.

One of the basic principles of trade is that both sides benefit. This is obvious when one country can produce a good or service that another cannot. For example, the UK cannot produce diamonds – we simply do not have deposits of that mineral. In South Africa, there are deposits of diamond. It makes sense for the UK to sell goods to South Africa which it cannot produce, in return for diamonds which we cannot produce.

It is less obvious that gains from trade can occur when a country is better at producing all sorts of different products. However, if countries specialise in those products or services in which they have relative advantage, there can be benefits to all from trade. For example, the UK could produce oranges. We could erect large glasshouses and have sophisticated heating, lighting and water devices to provide the conditions to produce oranges. However, it makes more sense for the UK to use those resources to produce something that we are better at growing, such as wheat. Spain, with its warm, sunny weather conditions, can grow oranges using fewer resources, while Britain focuses on producing wheat. Then the countries can swop oranges for wheat.

Poorer countries could benefit if they are encouraged to focus their resources on goods and services they can produce efficiently and then to trade them. Too many countries have set up barriers to trade that mean that the benefits of trade are not being gained. This will be dealt with in more detail in a later section.

There are two key terms that we need to be aware of with regard to trade. **Exports** refer to the sale of goods and services to another country, which lead to a payment or flow of money into the country. For example, if a UK business sells machinery to a firm in Germany, it will receive payment from the German company. **Imports** refer to the purchase of goods and services from another country, which lead to a payment to the other country and a flow of money out of the UK. For example, if a UK company purchases a supply of steel from a steel plant in Japan it will have to pay the Japanese firm. This represents an outflow of money from the UK to Japan.

You must remember that one country's exports are another country's imports. In this course, the discussion will normally be from a UK point of view. In this book, imports refer to UK businesses buying from abroad and exports refers to selling goods from the UK to other countries.

The benefits of trade

The benefits of trade include the following:

- It enables access to goods and services that cannot be produced in the home country. UK citizens have access to an incredible variety of goods and services. For example, 20 years ago, strawberries were only available for a few weeks a year. Now they are sold all year round.
- It enables access to goods and services at cheaper prices. The real price of many food and clothing items is now less than it was 30 years ago. This is largely due to competition from overseas.
- It helps to generate growth. Trade between nations helps to create growth in economic activity. This leads to rising standards of living. For many of the poorest nations on earth, increasing their trade with the rest of the world is one of the ways in which they can escape poverty. As economic growth occurs, governments can use the income from increased taxes to invest in health, education and other essential public services.

The costs of trade

Economists have shown that there are many benefits to trade. However, as with most things, there are costs and challenges.

Structural change

Many countries have industries that have developed over a period of time. One of the major challenges of the early twenty-first century to UK industry is the heavy competition from manufacturing companies in China. Manufacturing firms in the UK are finding it increasingly difficult to compete and many have closed down or been forced to relocate abroad to cope. It is estimated that 100,000 manufacturing jobs are being lost every year in the UK.

Manufacturing in China

Unemployment

As the structure of industry changes and international competition takes its toll, some people will lose their jobs. For example, many textile workers who were employed making clothing for **Marks & Spencer** found themselves out of work when the company decided to source its clothes from abroad in an effort to become more competitive in the retail clothing market.

In such cases, it is the availability of cheap imports that is seen as being the cause of the unemployment. This may lead to calls to restrict imports to protect jobs. Internationally, the fear of unemployment is one of the main reasons why it is proving so difficult to remove barriers to trade. For example, British and French farmers demand protection from cheaper imports of sugar, corn and wheat.

The need to protect infant industries

New businesses starting in a developing country often face difficulties in competing with businesses abroad. The government of developing countries sometimes impose some form of import barrier to help their new businesses to get established.

Protecting national culture

Some countries feel that imports can damage their cultural identity. For example, American culture has spread all over Europe. We have American films, many American TV programmes, plenty of American food, music and so on.

Investigation

The WTO and EU websites might be useful sources of information to help you with this investigation.

1 Identify and investigate an example of a trade dispute between countries. Explain what the dispute is about.
2 What is the main reason why the dispute has arisen and why?

Investigation

It has been said that UK manufacturing is losing around 100,000 jobs a year, much of it as a result of competition from cheaper manufactured goods in countries like China and India.

1 Prepare a report that assesses the costs and benefits of the UK seeking greater import protection of goods from these countries.

Investigation

1 Do some research around your home to find out where products around the home come from. Choose 20 such products that might include clothing, shoes and trainers, food products, electrical equipment, furniture and so on. Group the origins into regions – Europe, the USA, Asia, Africa, Australia.

2 Find out about the pattern of UK trade with the rest of the world. To what extent does the origin of the products in your home match that of UK trade? (You can find out about UK trade patterns through the Office for National Statistics website at www.statistics.gov.uk.)

34 Exchange rates, competitiveness and trade restrictions

The exchange rate

To succeed in selling goods to the world, businesses need to be internationally competitive. For example, a UK business selling chemicals to a customer in Germany will have to compete with the world's best chemical companies – most of whom are based in Germany. The UK firm will have to make sure that it keeps it quality high, costs low, efficiency high and prices competitive. That is the only way to maintain or increase sales. Such a business will be constantly watching what its competitors around the world are doing. If its labour costs rise faster than those in businesses in rival countries, the British firm may become uncompetitive. So all these things have to be monitored constantly.

Some of the costs that a business has to pay are within its control. For example, its workers may be demanding annual pay rises of 5 per cent. The business might only be willing to agree to this if staff agree to improve productivity levels. This can help the business to maintain its competitiveness abroad.

However, some things are outside its control. One of these is the exchange rate. The exchange rate is the price of one currency expressed in terms of another. It is how much a given amount of one currency (for example, pounds sterling) buys of another currency (for example, the Euro or dollar).

So, the exchange rate for the pound against the US dollar might be £1 = $1.90. This means that in giving up £1 you will get $1.9 dollars in return. It also means that at this exchange rate, $1 is worth around 53p.

The exchange rate is extremely important for businesses that trade abroad. UK firms importing goods from abroad must exchange pounds into the currency of the firm they are buying from.

If a UK importer buys 4,000 tonnes of oranges from a grower in the USA then the US grower will want paying in dollars. If the oranges are priced in US dollars at $95 per tonne, then the UK importer will have to exchange the equivalent amount of pounds to pay $380,000. If the exchange rate is £1 = $1.90, then they would have to exchange £200,000 to buy sufficient dollars.

UK firms selling goods abroad want to be paid in pounds. If a UK firm sells an insurance policy to cover a large office building in Germany, it will require payment in pounds. If the policy is priced in the UK at £400,000 per year and the exchange rate is £1 = €1.45, then the German firm will have to exchange €580,000 into pounds.

> To convert pounds to another currency, multiply the amount by the rate. If you are converting from another currency to pound sterling, divide the amount by the rate.
>
> For example, £50 in US dollars at an exchange rate of £1 = 1.90 would be 50 x 1.90 = $95. $100 expressed in pounds at the same exchange rate would be 100/1.90 = £52.63

The exchange rate is determined by the buying and selling of foreign currencies – in the case of sterling, the supply of and demand for pounds (£). Every day, billions of pounds worth of different currencies are traded on specialist markets, collectively known as the foreign exchange market. The foreign exchange market is made up of hundreds of traders who buy and sell currencies of all types on behalf of clients.

These clients might be businesses who are engaged in trade and need different currencies, banks and investors who are buying and selling stocks or shares around the world. Many transactions on the foreign exchange market are for speculative purposes. This means that traders may buy and sell currencies in the hope of making a profit. They will buy at one price and hope to sell at another thereby making a profit.

The exchange rate is constantly changing. The changes are usually small, but can make a huge difference where there is a lot of trade between two countries. For individual businesses, the changes in exchange rates mean that their competitiveness can be affected.

In the examples given above, the exchange rate was assumed to be £1 = $1.90 (US dollars) and £1 = €1.45 (Euros). What if the exchange rate between the pound and the Euro changed to £1 = €1.50? In the case of the UK firm selling the insurance policy to the German firm, the change in the exchange rate now means that the German firm has to give up €600,000 to pay for the insurance policy. The policy is now €20,000 more expensive for them.

If the exchange rate went from £1 = $1.90 to £1 = $1.88, we would say that the pound had 'fallen'. In this case, the pound is worth less in terms of dollars – you get fewer dollars for every pound.

If the pound goes up against other currencies, import prices fall but export prices rise. Firms importing goods and services from abroad can benefit from lower prices. Exporters, however, will face the prospect of foreign buyers having to pay more of their currency to get the same amount of pounds. To them, export prices have risen and UK exporters become less competitive.

If the pound falls against other currencies, import prices rise but export prices fall. Firms buying goods and services from abroad will now have to pay more pounds to buy the foreign currency. Import prices have risen. For exporters, a fall in the pound means that overseas customers can pay lower prices, which should boost the sales of UK exports.

Movements in exchange rates can be very significant for firms engaged in trade. It can affect their international competitiveness in serious ways and can, in some cases, put firms out of business. It depends, to a large extent, on how much of their business is traded abroad. However, a firm that sells products exclusively in the UK might not be affected by exchange rates at all.

Trade restrictions

While it is generally accepted that there are many benefits to trade (as outlined in Unit 33), many countries erect some form of trade restrictions to protect the economy of their own country. Trade restrictions may take one of three major forms: tariffs, quotas and non-tariff barriers.

Tariffs

A tariff is a tax on a good or service as it enters a country. It has the effect of increasing the price of a product and making it less competitive in the market. This is likely to cut its sales. For example, if a country imposed a tariff on cars from Japan, the Japanese firm would have to pay the government of that country a sum of money. This would effectively increase the cost of production for the Japanese firm and they would pass on the increased cost in the form of a higher price. This affects the competitiveness of the vehicle, as it is now more expensive.

The UK is a member of the European Union and is therefore not allowed to set its own barriers to trade. Instead, the EU sets tariffs on products coming into all EU countries.

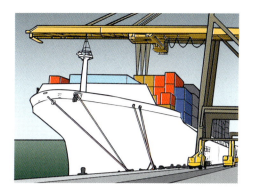

Quotas

A quota is a physical limit on the amount of goods coming into a country. For example, the EU set a quota on the number of imported shoes allowed in from China. When the quota was lifted on 1 January 2005, shoe imports from China rose by over 300 per cent.

Non-tariff barriers

Non-tariff barriers take many forms. They can be in the form of rules or regulations that a country lays down that make it harder for a business to comply. This may lead to them having to amend their production process and this can lead to higher costs as a result. Exhaust emissions from cars is one example. A UK firm selling cars to the USA might have to have far more stringent regulations on the level of emissions than is the case for the EU.

Other examples include documentation that may be required, or extremely long and complicated administrative procedures – in fact anything that would lead to life being made harder for an exporter or that might result in an increase in costs for the exporter. Any of these things just makes it more difficult – but not impossible – for a business to sell abroad.

Investigation

Select a country that trades with the EU but which is currently outside the EU. Assess the impact of the Common External Tariff on the country you have chosen.

Investigation

1 There have been a number of cases involving what is called the 'grey market' in recent years. Find out what is meant by this term.
2 Select one example of a case where the grey market has been an issue. Explain what the issue was about and what the result of any investigation into the dispute has been.
3 To what extent do you think the decision was justified?

35 Multinational companies

What is a multinational?

Multinationals are becoming an increasingly important part of the global economy. You will see many references to the process of 'globalisation'. Multinationals are part of that process.

   Globalisation is the spread of inter-connections between economies that effectively leads to a shrinking of the world in economic terms. A **multinational** is a company that has its headquarters in one country but may have many other departments, offices, outlets or factories in other countries.

   The existence of multinationals causes much debate. Some countries fear that the spread of multinationals might lead to a dilution of culture and tradition and this might be an argument against globalisation. However, there are plenty of people who would argue that multinationals bring tremendous benefits to countries around the world. As ever, there is a trade-off between the growth of multinational companies and the problems they might bring.

Why be a multinational?

There are very good economic reasons why companies grow and expand into different countries and continents.

Transport costs and distribution

Some businesses produce very bulky items that are not easy to transport across the globe, such as cement. As a result, the costs and difficulties of transporting make it sensible to produce in many countries, rather than to export from one country.

Avoiding trade barriers

Countries operating outside the EU have to pay a tariff if they wish to sell their products inside the EU. For Japanese companies like Honda and Nissan, the costs involved and the restrictions on their exports would be significant. However, they have overcome some of the problems by setting up factories in the UK, which means they can manufacture goods within the EU.

Security of supplies or markets

Businesses may find that it is sensible to locate in different countries to be nearer to the markets they serve. For example, it might not be very easy for McDonalds to have one central factory producing burgers in the USA to ship to every one of its 30,000 plus restaurants in around 120 countries!

Lower costs

Setting up operations in some countries might enable a firm to be able to secure lower costs of production. This may be because labour costs, raw materials or access to land might be cheaper. Some critics of multinationals argue that they set up in countries where health and safety regulations are lighter, as this could also reduce the costs of production quite significantly for many firms.

The benefits of multinationals

Economic growth

Multinationals have the resources to invest heavily in the development of new factories. Such an investment might be expected to feed its way into the local economy. Local people may become employed by the multinational. This provides them with an income which they spend in other local businesses. This, in turn, encourages new firms to start up to take advantage of the developments in the economy.

Employment

Many multinationals are prepared to provide training and opportunities for education which may not otherwise be available. They might invest money in local schools, colleges or universities to help provide the supply of skilled labour that they require. This will help the country's economic growth. Such skills may be transferable and lead to a more mobile and flexible workforce that can adapt to change and learn new skills more quickly.

Tax revenue

Multinationals generate wealth within a country and should be subject to that country's tax laws. As a result, not only should income taxes from newly employed labour rise, but also tax revenues received from the company itself. Critics, however, argue that multinational companies such as Virgin are too good at minimising the tax they pay.

Improvements in infrastructure

Multinationals might need more modern communications networks like roads, rail links, airports and phone networks if they decide to invest in an area. Part of the investment in building a factory, for example, might also include contributions to building communications networks. This is of benefit to the community as a whole.

The costs of multinationals

In some cases, the costs of multinationals are hidden in the supposed benefits. The extent of the benefits depend on a variety of factors.

- Multinationals may improve local employment levels, but some employ local people in low-skilled jobs and reserve the skilled work for staff that they bring in from their own country. The number of new jobs may be further limited by the fact that the plants that are built might be very capital intensive – lots of machinery and equipment and relatively small numbers of workers.

- Some multinationals might look to locate in countries where they get tax advantages – grants and subsidies designed to encourage them to invest. This, along with the employment of highly skilled accountants might mean that the contributions to tax revenue of the country might not be as much as expected.

- There are also suggestions that some of the multinationals are very powerful organisations. They might be so powerful that they can exert influence on governments to gain tax benefits or concessions that might benefit the multinational, but not the country.

- There have been suggestions that the activities of some multinational firms cause significant damage to the environment. Pollution of land and air, overuse of local essential resources like water, a failure to consider health and safety, dumping of waste and so on might all be problems that arise from the activities of multinationals.

Pollution caused by mining

- The wealth created by a multinational in a country might not stay in that country. Profits made may be returned to the country where the company's headquarters are based. As a result, the wealth created may not be as great for the country as expected.

It is important when analysing and evaluating the activities of multinationals that you find evidence to support your arguments. The opponents of multinationals may present information that is high on emotion but light on fact. Equally, you have to be very sceptical about believing every claim made by multinationals. Good economics is based on fact, not opinion.

Investigation

1 Choose a company that is a multinational. Find out where the company has its global operations and present this information in a suitable format.
2 Identify and explain the possible reasons why the company operates in the countries it does. Which is the most important reason for their multinational status and why?

Investigation

The website of the independent research and publishing group Corporate Watch (at www.corporatewatch.org.uk) contains information about a wide range of multinationals in different industries. It claims to offer an alternative view about the social and environmental impact of the activities of multinationals.

1 Visit the Corporate Watch website and research one multinational of your choice. Then visit the multinational's own website and do some comparative research on what they say about their activities.
2 Prepare a report assessing the impact of the multinational on society and the environment.

36 Trade or aid?

What is the best way of helping poor countries to escape poverty? This is a fiercely debated topic with no easy answers. Some argue that the best way to help is to provide aid – donations of money equipment and labour resources. Others argue that aid merely leads to dependence – the population comes to rely on it and it does not help them to be able to help themselves. They suggest that encouraging trade is a more effective method of helping to solve the problems of poverty.

The trade argument

We have seen that there are a number of benefits to trade. Poor countries have problems selling their products abroad. At the same time, they have little power to prevent richer countries flooding their markets with products. If rich countries made trade fairer, poorer countries would be able to sell their products abroad, generating income and wealth.

The problems faced by poor countries in this respect are very large. In countries like Brazil, Mali, Burkino Faso and Benin, cotton is an important product. Over 10 million people rely on cotton production for their livelihoods. The USA also produces cotton. The US government provides $4bn worth of subsidies to cotton producers in the USA. The total subsidy is more than the whole GDP of Burkino Faso and about

three times the amount that the USA sends annually in aid to Africa as a whole.

African cotton growers argue that the US subsidy causes the world price of cotton to fall. The subsidy encourages US growers to expand production; supply increases and prices fall. African growers are having to compete without the subsidies. As a result, the price of cotton is not enough to cover their costs.

Removing the subsidy to US growers would be the most effective help that people who rely on cotton for their living could receive. This would help to get the price of cotton rising and enable growers in countries like Burkino Faso to sell their cotton to the USA. Removing trade barriers would, according to the World Trade Organisation, generate an extra £280 billion in global revenues over about the next ten years, and many poor countries would benefit from this increase in economic activity.

The aid argument

International aid can be given to a country by another country, by a group of countries or by international institutions and banks. There are arguments for and against giving aid.

The case for aid

Aid can be given for a variety of reasons, and used in a variety of ways.

To invest in improving the economy

This might be used for infrastructure projects like buildings, roads, factories bridges, communication links, energy supplies, water supplies and so on. It might also be used for investing in health and education services to improve the quality of human capital.

Political support

Aid might be given as a means of showing support to a political ruler or regime. Over the past 20 years both the UK and the USA provided aid to Iraq while Saddam Hussein was the ruler. This was as a means of maintaining support and influence in the region. In some cases it might be that such aid helps to provide contracts and work for companies from the country who are offering the aid.

Moral duty

Some would argue that rich nations have a moral duty to provide help for poorer countries.

To help in times of disaster

Many poorer countries are prone to natural disasters like flood, drought, earthquake, hurricanes and so on. When these strike and people are in desperate need of immediate help and support, aid might be one of the few ways to provide such help and assistance.

The case against aid

There are arguments against the provision of aid, however.

Uncertainty as to how it is used

Millions of pounds have been provided to poor countries over the years. Sometimes, clear records are not kept about how the funds have been used. In some cases, the funds may not reach their intended target. They might end up being used on projects that are of little benefit to the economy, or even be used in the personal projects of corrupt leaders.

Difficulty in budgeting effectively

Aid flows are not necessarily regular or reliable – the funds available might depend on lots of factors. Governments faced with the difficulties that many poor countries face need reliable and regular sources of funds to enable them to budget over long periods of time. It might be many years before any long-term benefits of investment are realised.

Dependency

It is argued that countries who receive aid come to rely on it and do not learn to manage their own economy. In many cases, aid might only be a short-term option and it does not solve the root causes of the problems that countries face.

It is likely that the answer to the problems faced by many poorer countries lies somewhere between the two. In some cases, aid will be appropriate but in others opening up markets to allow countries to trade more freely might be necessary. If you are investigating such an issue, you will need to consider the particular circumstances of the country concerned. Not every country has the same cause of poverty, not every country has the same problems and as such the solutions are also, therefore, likely to be very different.

Investigation

Take an example of a recent case where aid has been given to a country. This might have been as a result of a natural disaster or because of drought, famine or conflict. Who were responsible for giving the aid in the case you have selected? To what extent does the aid programme appear to have been successful?

Investigation

Select one country where there is evidence that there is widespread poverty and economic problems. Explain what the main problems facing the country are in dealing with poverty. What strategies would you recommend the country adopt to solve its problems – explain your reasoning.

Investigation

The WTO claims that the global economy would be boosted by as much as £280 billion if global trade barriers could be reduced. Using appropriate economic analysis, explain how the reduction of global trade barriers might trigger economic growth. What would be the most important factor that would contribute to economic growth?

Investigation

Choose a product like cotton or bananas where there have been disputes over the levels of trade protection given to producers. Explain how the removal of such trade barriers would help poor countries to be more competitive in world markets. To what extent would the removal of such trade barriers help poor countries to escape from poverty?

Index